JAVA

MIKE McGRATH

In easy steps is an imprint of Computer Step
Southfield Road . Southam
Warwickshire CV47 0FB . United Kingdom
www.ineasysteps.com

Notice of Liability
Every effort has been made to ensure that this book contains accurate and current information. However, Computer Step and the author shall not be liable for any loss or damage suffered by readers as a result of any information contained herein.

Trademarks
Java and all Java-based trademarks and logos including the Java Coffee Cup and Duke are trademarks or registered trademarks of Sun Microsystems, Inc. All other trademarks are acknowledged as belonging to their respective companies.

Printed and bound in the United Kingdom

ISBN 1-84078-259-5

Contents

Introducing Java

Welcome to the exciting world of Java programming. This first chapter introduces Java with guidance on how to download and install the Java Software Development Kit. A simple first program demonstrates how easy Java programming really is.

Covers

Chapter One

Introduction

The Java programming language was first developed in 1990 by an engineer at Sun Microsystems named James Gosling.

He was unhappy using the C++ programming language so he created a new language that he called "Oak", after the oak tree that he could see from his office window.

As the popularity of the World Wide Web grew Sun recognized that Gosling's language could be developed to run applications on a web page.

The language was renamed "Java", simply because the name sounded cool, and was made freely available by Sun in 1995.

Developers around the world quickly adopted this exciting new language and, because of its modular design, began to create new features that could be added to the core language.

Many of these additional features were incorporated into Java when it was updated in 1998 and renamed "Java 2".

Subsequent updates have enhanced some multimedia features and added support for the Linux operating system.

There is no truth in the rumor that "JAVA" stands for "Just Another Vague Acronym".

The essence of Java is a library of files called "classes" that each contain small pieces of ready-made proven code.

Any of these classes can be added into a new program, like bricks in a wall, so that only a relatively small amount of new code ever needs to be written.

This saves the program author a vast amount of time and largely explains the huge popularity of Java programming.

Also this modular arrangement makes it much easier to identify any errors than would a single large program.

This book demonstrates a first simple Java program over the next few pages before explaining, by example, the basic mechanics of the Java language.

After developing an understanding of the Java language the remaining chapters give full examples of how to incorporate many of the ready-made classes into new Java programs.

In order to create any Java program the Java class libraries need to be available on the local computer system. These are all contained in a freely available package called the Java 2 SDK (Software Development Kit) that also includes all the tools needed to build and run Java programs.

The Java programs in this book use version 1.4.2 of the Java 2 SDK Standard Edition that can be downloaded from Sun Microsystems' website at **http://java.sun.com**.

The Sun download page also features other packages but only the Java 2 SDK is required now.

The Java 2 SDK Standard Edition is suitable for computers running on Microsoft Windows 95, 98, Me, NT, 2000 and XP. Separate versions of the SDK are available for computers running on Linux or Solaris operating systems.

Selecting the installation link for your platform starts the Java 2 SDK installation – this may take some time, depending on the speed of your connection. Full documentation for the Java 2 SDK is available as a separate download. This is not initially required for the examples given in this book and may be downloaded later after you have become more familiar with Java.

Installing the Java SDK

Run the downloaded SDK executable file and, when prompted, either accept the default installation path or enter a location where the Java files are to be installed, such as "C:\Java".

The installer's Custom Setup dialog box will then offer a choice of components that may be installed. Only the Development Tools component is essential to start programming with this book so all other components may be excluded from the installation to save disk space.

Demos may be installed if disk space permits and are useful to demonstrate some aspects of Java in action.

Source files are merely used to create the Java language.

Following component selection the installation will automatically complete with all the necessary Java class libraries and tools being installed at the chosen location.

Start out by installing just the minimum options to avoid confusion.

![Java 2 SDK, SE v1.4.2 - Custom Setup dialog box]

Java 2 SDK, SE v1.4.2 - Custom Setup

Custom Setup

Select the program features you want installed.

Select optional features to install from the list below. You can change your choice of features after installation by using the Add/Remove Programs utility

- Development Tools
- Demos
- Source Code
- Public Java Runtime Environment

Feature Description

The Java 2 SDK, SE v1.4.2, including private j2re1.4.2. This will require 120 MB on your hard drive.

Install to:
C:\Java\

Change...

InstallShield

< Back   Next >   Cancel

The tools to compile and run Java programs are normally operated from a Command Prompt, such as C:\>. They are located in the "bin" folder of the Java installation directory and can be made available from anywhere on the computer by adding their location to the system path.

*On older versions of Windows the SDK can be made globally available by editing the **autoexec.bat** file to add the location of the Java tools at the end of the SET PATH line.*

On Windows XP navigate through **Start > Control Panel > System** then click the **Advanced** tab and click the **Environment Variables** button. In the Environment Variables dialog select the **System Variable** named "Path", then click the **Edit** button. Add the address of the Java bin directory to the end of the list in the **Variable Value** field. For instance, add **C:\Java\bin;** if you chose to install the SDK at **C:\Java**.

Click on the **OK** buttons to close the Environment Variables dialog then reboot the system to apply the new Path setting.

To test that the Java tools are now globally accessible open a Command Prompt window and type **java -version** at the prompt. The SDK should respond with version information like this:

```
C:\>java -version
java version "1.4.2"
Java(TM) 2 Runtime Environment, Standard Edition
Java HotSpot(TM) Client VM (build 1.4.2-b28)

C:\>_
```

If Java responds with a **Bad command or file name** message this means that the command was mis-typed or the system cannot find the files that are needed to run Java programs.

Check the Path settings given in the instructions above then reboot the system and retry the test.

When Java responds to the **java -version** command correctly the system is ready to start writing Java programs.

A first Java program

All Java programs start as text files that are later used to create "class" files which are the actual runnable programs. This means that Java programs can be written in any simple text editor such as Windows Notepad application.

The Java code that is entered below into Notepad will generate the traditional first program output of "Hello World".

```
Hello.java - Notepad
File  Edit  Format  View  Help

public class Hello
{
  public static void main (String[] args)
  {
    System.out.println("Hello World");
  }
}
```

Programs are Java "classes" and the first line of this code defines the name of this program as "Hello". It is important to note that Java is a case-sensitive language where "Hello" and "hello" are two different programs.

Java program files are saved with their exact program name, matching character case, and with the file extension ".java". So the above program is saved as a file named "Hello.java".

Create a new folder at C:\MyJava in which to save program files.

MyJava

File Edit View Favorites Tools Help

Back · Search Folders

File and Folder Tasks

Make a new folder
Publish this folder to the Web
Share this folder

Hello.java

The program code on the facing page can be broken down into three separate parts to understand it more clearly.

The Program Container

```
public class Hello { }
```

The program name is declared following the "public class" keywords and followed by a pair of curly brackets.

All of the program code that defines the Hello class will be contained within these curly brackets.

The Main Method

```
public static void main (String[] args) { }
```

This fearsome looking line is the standard code that is used to define the starting point of nearly all Java programs.

All stand-alone Java programs must have a main method. Java applets are different and their format is explained later.

It will be used in most examples throughout this book exactly as it appears above so it may usefully be memorized.

The code declares a method named "main" that will contain the actual program instructions within its curly brackets.

Keywords "public static void" prefix the method name to define how it may be used and are explained in detail later.

The code "(String[] args)" is useful when passing values to the method and is also fully explained later in this book.

The Statement

```
System.out.println( "Hello World" );
```

Statements are actual instructions to perform program tasks and must always end with a semicolon.

A method may contain many statements inside its curly brackets to form a "statement block" but here a single statement instructs the program to output a line of text.

Compiling and running programs

Before a Java program can run it must first be compiled into a "class" file by the Java compiler. This is located in the Java directory **bin** folder and is an application named **javac.exe**.

At a command prompt simply type **javac** then hit the **Return** key in order to reveal the Java compiler options.

To compile a program at a command prompt type **javac** followed by a space then the path and file name of the file to be compiled, for instance **C:\>javac C:\MyJava\Hello.java**.

Alternatively change the prompt location to the directory containing the source file. Then type **javac** followed by a space then the full file name of the file to be compiled.

```
C:\MyJava>javac Hello.java

C:\MyJava>_
```

Use the "cd" command to navigate to the source files directory or create a desktop shortcut to open a command prompt window in that directory.

If the compiler finds errors in the code it will halt and display a helpful report indicating the nature of the error. Typically errors are due to incorrect code syntax or, where the compiler cannot find the source file, due to an incorrectly entered file name or path.

If the compiler does not find errors it will create a new file with the program name and with the file extension ".class".

When the Java compiler completes compilation of a program source file focus returns to a standard command prompt without confirming that the compilation was successful.

Now the actual compiled program can finally be run.

The SDK tool used to run Java programs is an application called **java.exe** located in the Java directory bin folder.

At a command prompt simply type **java** then hit the Return key in order to reveal the Java interpreter options.

To run a program at a command prompt type **java** followed by a space then the path and file name of the program, for instance **C:\>java C:\MyJava\Hello**.

Alternatively change the prompt location to the directory containing the class file. Then type **java** followed by a space then the program name only.

In this example the command prompt is located in the directory containing the class file so the simple command **java Hello** will run the Hello program.

Do not type the file extension when running Java programs.

```
Command Prompt                                    _ □ ✕

C:\MyJava>java Hello
Hello World

C:\MyJava>_
```

When a program runs, the Java interpreter reads the program class file and executes its instructions.

In this case the statement contained in the program's main method will output the line of text "Hello World".

After the program has completed executing the program instructions, focus returns to a standard command prompt.

Integrated development environments

The continual switching between text editor and command line when creating Java programs can become tedious.

An Integrated Development Environment (IDE) is a piece of software that can make the process more convenient.

There are many IDEs available for Java but all provide an intrinsic text editor, in which to write the code, and a graphical means to compile and run the code.

This not only makes life more pleasant but speeds development time and avoids the use of command lines.

Most IDE text editors offer syntax highlighting that will apply different colors to each piece of the program code to denote its relevance. For instance, all keywords that are recognized as part of the Java language might be bright red.

Another benefit offered by IDEs is an integrated debugger that can help to find any errors in the program code.

Several Java IDEs are visual development tools that can very quickly build a program interface by allowing components to be dragged into a base window.

The IDE application will then automatically generate the appropriate code to add that component to the program.

Probably the most popular visual Java IDE is the award-winning Borland JBuilder application. This is a comprehensive Rapid Application Development (RAD) tool for Java programmers. Further details on Borland JBuilder can be found on the web at **http://www.inprise.com/jbuilder**.

RAD IDEs are mostly useful for experienced programmers who understand the Java basics. This is because the generated code still needs to be modified to make the components perform actions.

The Java non-visual IDE used throughout this book is the excellent JPadPro application that is introduced over the following pages.

The JPadPro IDE

JPadPro is a non-visual Java IDE that allows the user to write, compile and run Java programs from a single Windows interface without the need to type command line instructions.

The JPadPro IDE by Modelworks is available for download from their website at **http://www.modelworks.com** and may be freely used for an evaluation period. Registration is inexpensive and worthwhile for anyone writing Java code.

Installation of JPadPro is straightforward and should automatically detect the Java 2 SDK **bin** directory so that the IDE is ready for immediate use.

The illustration below shows the JPadPro interface loaded with the Hello program from earlier in this chapter. A text editor displays the source code and the output panel at the bottom shows the results when the program has run.

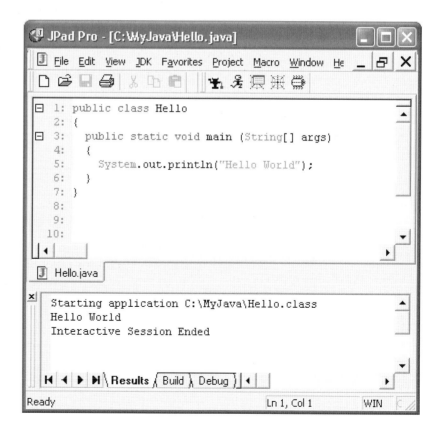

Creating programs with JPadPro

To create a new Java source file in JPadPro select **File** then **New** on the menu or click on the ⬜ new file icon.

This will open a "New" dialog box that allows selection of the file type – so choose "Java file" then click the OK button.

New

Java Applet	OK
Java file	
Java file - Blank	Cancel
Java file - Custom	
Java file - JUnit Test Case	Types...
Java file - JUnit Test Suite	
Java file - Simple class	
Java file - Simple public class	
JavaScript file	

The "New Java File" dialog will open to allow the name and destination of the new file to be specified.

Enter a name for the program in the "Class name" text field.

Check that the path location is suitable then click the "Create File" button to make the new Java source file.

It is convention to use uppercase for the first letter of Java program names.

New Java File

Class name:

Hello

Full path:

C:\MyJava\Hello.java

[Create Untitled] [Create File] [Cancel]

When the text editor window opens to reveal the contents of the new Java source file JPadPro adds a comment block at the top of the page and code declaring the program name. Program names are always declared with exactly the name given to that Java file including correct capitalization. The program code is added in the text editor then compiled to make a class file by clicking the toolbar **Compile** button.

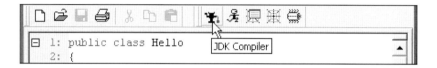

On the menu under View – Preferences ensure that the option "Always show choose application dialog" is not checked.

The build progress is shown in the bottom output panel and helpful messages are displayed for any errors that are found. When the file compiles successfully the simple message "Finished" confirms that the program is now ready to run. Simply click on the toolbar **Run** button to run the program.

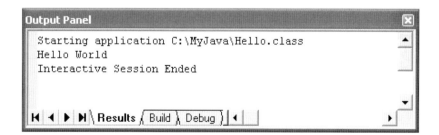

The JPadPro output panel will identify the program path then display its output and confirm when the program ends.

Output Panel

```
Starting application C:\MyJava\Hello.class
Hello World
Interactive Session Ended
```

Results Build Debug

Comments and backslash

It is useful, and good practice, when writing Java code, to add comments that describe what each piece of code is doing.

This makes the code easier to understand when it is revisited after several months or when it is viewed by someone else.

The Java compiler sees any text between // and the end of that line as a single-line comment which it ignores. Also any text, on one or more lines, between /* and */ is ignored.

Spaces, tabs and new lines in the code are collectively known as "whitespace". This too is ignored by the compiler so code may be formatted and indented to make it more readable.

The backslash character has a special meaning in strings – inside quoted text strings **\n** will force a line-break in the output and **\t** will add a tab spacing to the output. It is also useful as **\"** will allow quotation marks to be used inside strings without prematurely terminating the string.

Here these features are added to the Hello program:

Hello.java

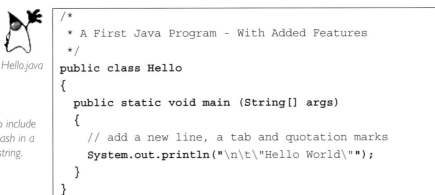

```
/*
 * A First Java Program - With Added Features
 */
public class Hello
{
  public static void main (String[] args)
  {
    // add a new line, a tab and quotation marks
    System.out.println("\n\t\"Hello World\"");
  }
}
```

Use \\ to include a backslash in a quoted string.

Output Panel   ☒

Starting application C:\MyJava\Hello.class

    "Hello World"
Interactive Session Ended

⏮ ◀ ▶ ⏭ \ Results ╱ Build ╲ Debug ╱ ◀   ▶

Variables and operators

This chapter shows how to store program data inside containers called "variables". The different types of variable are demonstrated together with all the "operators" that can be used to manipulate data in a Java program.

Covers

Chapter Two

Creating a variable

A "variable" is simply a container in which a value may be stored for subsequent manipulation within a program.

The stored value may be changed by the program as it executes its instructions – hence the term "variable".

Java is a "strongly typed language" that must specify when creating variables the type of data that may be stored inside.

To create a variable, and assign a value, use this syntax:

```
dataType variableName = value ;
```

Text strings must always be surrounded by double quotes – to denote the String's start and finish.

A common type of Java variable is used to store text, as a string of characters, and is called a "String" data type.

The example code below creates a String variable called "str" that can be used by the program to refer to the stored text.

This program writes out the original variable value, then assigns a new value that is written out on the next line:

FirstVar.java

```java
public class FirstVar
{
  public static void main(String[] args)
  {
    String str = "First value";
    System.out.println(str);
    str = "Second value";
    System.out.println(str);
  }
}
```

This program is saved in the C:\MyJava folder as FirstVar.java.

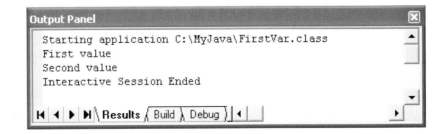

```
Output Panel                                    ☒

  Starting application C:\MyJava\FirstVar.class  ▲
  First value
  Second value
  Interactive Session Ended
                                                 ▼
 ⊮ ◄ ► ⊯ \ Results ⟨ Build ⟩ Debug ⟩| ◄ |      ►
```

When naming Java variables the name chosen should reflect the contents and must adhere to certain naming restrictions.

All variable names should start with either a letter or the underscore character or a $ symbol. Numbers may be used elsewhere in the name but spaces are not allowed.

So "myVar1", "_myVar" and "$myVar" are all valid names.

The table below lists the Java keywords that have special meaning in Java and cannot be used as variable names:

The "goto" and "const" keywords are not currently used but are nonetheless still reserved.

abstract	else	interface	String
boolean	extends	long	super
break	false	native	switch
byte	final	new	synchronized
case	finally	null	this
catch	float	package	throw
char	for	private	throws
class	goto	protected	transient
const	if	public	true
continue	implements	return	try
default	import	short	void
do	instanceof	static	volatile
double	int	strictfp	while

It is customary to begin variable names with a lowercase letter and class program names with an uppercase letter.

If the variable name consists of more than one word they are joined together and all but the first word start in uppercase.

Variable data types

The most commonly used data types that are declared when creating Java variables are listed in the table below:

All data type keywords start with lowercase except String which starts with an uppercase "S".

Keyword	Description of Data Type
char	A single Unicode character
String	A string of Unicode characters
int	An integer number from -2.14 billion to 2.14 billion
float	A floating-point number with a decimal point
boolean	A boolean value of true or false

In addition to these common data types Java provides more specialized data types for use in exacting circumstances.

These specialized data types that may be used to declare precise numeric variables are listed in the following table:

The compiler will report an error if the program attempts to assign the wrong type of data to a variable.

Keyword	Description of Data Type
byte	Integer number from -128 to 127
short	Integer number from -32,768 to 32,767
long	Positive or negative integer exceeding 2.14 billion
double	A long floating-point number for double precision

The circumstances where specialized data type variables are useful occur more in advanced Java programs but they are listed here for completeness.

When starting out in Java programming it is simpler to concentrate only on the common data type variables.

To avoid confusion the examples in this book will only use variables of the common data types listed in the top table.

The program below creates a Java variable with each of the most common data types then displays each stored value:

Variables.java

```java
public class Variables
{
  public static void main (String[] args)
  {
    // declare & initialize each variable type
    char chr = 'M';
    String str = "Java in easy steps";
    int num = 12345;
    float dec = 7f;
    boolean flg = false;

    // display value stored in each variable
    System.out.println("Character is " + chr);
    System.out.println("Text string is " + str);
    System.out.println("Integer number is " + num);
    System.out.println("Decimal number is " + dec);
    System.out.println("Boolean flag is " + flg);
  }
}
```

The character assigned to a char variable is always enclosed in single quotes – not double quotes.

The boolean true and false values are keywords that should not be enclosed in quotation marks.

Output Panel ☒

```
Starting application C:\MyJava\Variables.class
Character is M
Text string is Java in easy steps
Integer number is 12345
Decimal number is 7.0
Boolean flag is false
Interactive Session Ended
```

Results / Build \ Debug

It is important to notice that numbers assigned to float variables should always be suffixed by "f" or "F".

This is to denote that they must be treated as floating-point numbers rather than integer or double data types.

Arithmetical operators

The arithmetical operators commonly used in Java are listed in the table below, along with the operations that they perform:

Operator	Operation
+	Addition (and concatenates strings)
-	Subtraction
*	Multiplication
/	Division
%	Modulus
++	Increment
- -	Decrement

Notice that the "+" operator has two types of operation depending on the given operands. It will add together two numeric values and give the result of the addition. It will also join together two string values and return the concatenated string, as in the example on the facing page.

The modulus operator will divide the first given number by the second given number and return the remainder of the operation. This is most useful to determine if a number has an odd or even value.

The increment ++ and decrement -- operators alter the given value by 1 and return the resulting new value. These are most commonly used to count iterations in a loop.

All the other operators act as you would expect but care should be taken to bracket expressions where more than one operator is being used, to clarify the operations:

```
a = b * c - d % e / f ;           \\ This is unclear

a = (b * c) - ((d % e) / f );     \\ This is clear
```

The program below demonstrates each of the arithmetical operators from the opposite page in practical use:

Arithmetic.java

```java
public class Arithmetic
{
  public static void main (String[] args)
  {
    // create variables, initialize & operate
    int addNum = 20 + 30;
    String addStr = "I love " + "Java";
    float sub = 35.75f - 28.25f;
    int mul = 8 * 50;
    int mod =  65 % 2;
    int incr = 5 ; incr = ++incr;
    int decr = 5 ; decr = --decr;

    // display results
    System.out.println("Added numbers total " +addNum);
    System.out.println("Concatenated string is"+addStr);
    System.out.println("Subtraction result : " +sub);
    System.out.println("Multiplication result: " +mul);
    System.out.println("Modulus result:" +mod);
    System.out.println("Increment result: " +incr);
    System.out.println("Decrement result: " +decr);
  }
}
```

The increment and decrement operators may also be used following the operand. Note that in those cases they will perform the operation but only return the unoperated value.

Output Panel ☒

```
Starting application C:\MyJava\Arithmetic.class
Added numbers total 50
Concatenated string is I love Java
Subtraction result : 7.5
Multiplication result: 400
Modulus result:1
Increment result: 6
Decrement result: 4
Interactive Session Ended
|
```

◄ ◄ ► ►◄ \ Results / Build \ Debug } ◄

Logical operators

The logical operators most commonly used in Java programming are listed in the table below:

Operator	Operation
&&	Logical AND
||	Logical OR
!	Logical NOT

The logical operators are used with operands that have the boolean values of true or false, or are values that can convert to true or false.

The logical "&&" operator will evaluate two operands and return true only if both operands themselves are true. Otherwise the "&&" operator will return false.

This is used in "conditional branching" where the direction of a Java program is determined by testing two conditions.
If both conditions are satisfied the program will go in a certain direction, otherwise it will take a different direction.

Unlike the "&&" operator that needs both operands to be true the "||" operator will evaluate its two operands and return true if either one of the operands itself returns true. If neither operand returns true then "||" will return false. This is useful in Java programming to perform a certain action if either one of two test conditions has been met.

The third logical operator "!" is a unary operator that is used before a single operand. It returns the inverse value of the given operand so if the variable "a" had a value of true then "!a" would have a value of false. It is useful in Java programs to toggle the value of a variable in successive loop iterations with a statement like "a=!a". This ensures that on each pass the value is changed, like flicking a light switch on and off.

The program below demonstrates how boolean values may be tested with each of the logical operators shown opposite:

Logical.java

```
public class Logical
{
  public static void main (String[] args)
  {
    // declare & initialize test variables
    boolean a = true, b = false;

    boolean c1 = ( a && a );   // test if both are true
    boolean c2 = ( a && b );
    boolean c3 = ( b && b );

    boolean c4 = ( a || a );   // test if either is true
    boolean c5 = ( a || b );
    boolean c6 = ( b || b );

    boolean c7 = !a;                // invert initial values
    boolean c8 = !b;

    // display the results
    System.out.println("AND:\n1:"+c1+" 2:"+c2+" 3:"+c3);
    System.out.println("OR: \n4:"+c4+" 5:"+c5+" 6:"+c6);
    System.out.println("NOT:\n7:"+c7+" 8:"+c8);
  }
}
```

Notice how two variables of the same type can be declared together if separated by a comma.

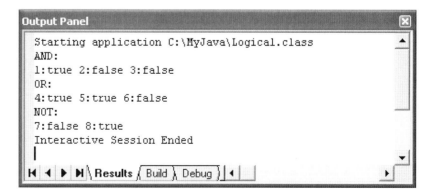

Output Panel

```
Starting application C:\MyJava\Logical.class
AND:
1:true 2:false 3:false
OR:
4:true 5:true 6:false
NOT:
7:false 8:true
Interactive Session Ended
```

H ◄ ► H \ Results / Build \ Debug / ◄

Assignment operators

The operators that are commonly used in Java to assign values are listed in the table below. All except the simple assign operator "=" are a shorthand form of a longer expression – so each equivalent is also given for clarity.

Operator	Example	Equivalent
=	a = b	a = b
+=	a += b	a = a + b
-=	a -= b	a = a - b
*=	a *= b	a = a * b
/=	a /= b	a = a / b
%=	a %= b	a = a % b

The equality operator compares values and is explained fully, with examples, on page 32.

It is important to regard the "=" operator to mean "assign" rather than "equals" to avoid confusion with the equality operator "==".

In the example above the variable named "a" is assigned the value that is contained in the variable named "b" – so that value becomes the new value stored in the "a" variable.

The "+=" operator is useful to add a value onto an existing value that is stored in a variable.

In the table example the "+=" operator first adds the value contained in variable "a" to the value contained in the variable named "b". It then assigns the result to become the new value stored in the "a" variable.

All the other operators in the table work in the same way by making the arithmetical operation between the two values first, then assigning the result to the first variable to become its new stored value.

The program below illustrates how the assignment operators can be used to concatenate strings and manipulate numbers:

Assignment.java

Assignment of the wrong data type to a variable will cause an error.

```java
public class Assignment
{
  public static void main (String[] args)
  {
    String a = "Fantastic", b= " Java"; a += b;
    System.out.println("Add & Assign String: " + a);

    int c = 8, d = 4; c += d;
    System.out.println("Add & Assign Integer: " + c);

    float e = 7.5F, f = 2.25F; e -= f;
    System.out.println("Subtract & Assign Float: " + e);

    int g = 8, h = 4; g *= h;
    System.out.println("Multiply & Assign Integer: " +g);

    int i = 8, j = 4; i /= j;
    System.out.println("Divide & Assign Integer: " + i);

    int k = 8, l = 4; k %= l;
    System.out.println("Modulus & Assign Integer: " + k);
  }
}
```

Output Panel ⊠

```
Starting application C:\MyJava\Assignment.class
Add & Assign String: Fantastic Java
Add & Assign Integer: 12
Subtract & Assign Float: 5.25
Multiply & Assign Integer: 32
Divide & Assign Integer: 2
Modulus & Assign Integer: 0
Interactive Session Ended
|
```
|◄ ◄ ► ►|\ Results ⟨ Build ⟩ Debug ⟩|◄ | | ►|

Comparison operators

The operators that are commonly used in Java programming to compare two values are all listed in the table below:

Operator	Comparative Test
==	Equality
!=	Inequality
>	Greater than
<	Less than
>=	Greater than or equal to
<=	Less than or equal to

An example of the "less than" operator "<" in a Java loop statement can be found on page 40.

The equality operator "==" compares two operands and will return true if both are equal in value. If both are the same number they are equal, or if both are strings containing the same characters in the same positions they are equal. Boolean operands that are both true, or both false, are equal.

Conversely the "!=" operator returns true if two operands are not equal using the same rules as the "==" operator.

Equality and inequality operators are useful in testing the state of two variables to perform conditional branching.

The "greater than" operator compares two operands and will return true if the first is greater in value than the second.

The "less than" operator makes the same comparison but returns true if the first operand is less in value than the second.

Adding the "=" operator after a "greater than" or "less than" operator makes it also return true if the two operands are exactly equal in value.

The "greater than" operator ">" is frequently used to test the value of a countdown value in a loop.

The program below illustrates how the comparison operators can be used to compare strings and numbers:

Comparison.java

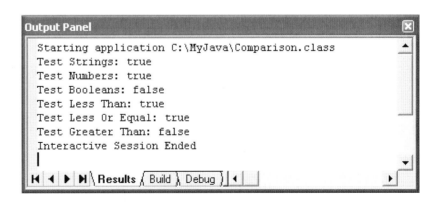

Notice that the capitalization should also match to make strings equal.

```java
public class Comparison
{
  public static void main (String[] args)
  {
    boolean testStr = ( "Java" == "Java" );
    System.out.println("Test Strings: " + testStr);

    boolean testNum = ( 1.785 == 1.785 );
    System.out.println("Test Numbers: " + testNum);

    boolean testBool = ( true != true );
    System.out.println("Test Booleans: " + testBool);

    boolean testLess = ( 100 < 200 );
    System.out.println("Test Less Than: " + testLess);

    boolean LessEq = ( 100 <= 100 );
    System.out.println("Test Less Or Equal: " + LessEq);

    boolean testGtr = ( -1 > 1 );
    System.out.println("Test Greater Than: " + testGtr);
  }
}
```

Output Panel ☒

```
Starting application C:\MyJava\Comparison.class
Test Strings: true
Test Numbers: true
Test Booleans: false
Test Less Than: true
Test Less Or Equal: true
Test Greater Than: false
Interactive Session Ended
|
```

◄◄ ◄ ► ►◄ \ Results / Build \ Debug] ◄ | ►

Conditional operator

The Java programmer's favorite test operator is probably the conditional operator. This first evaluates an expression for a true or false value then executes one of two given statements depending on the result of the evaluation.

The conditional operator has this syntax:

```
(test-expression) ? if-true-do-this : if-false-do-this ;
```

This operator is used to execute Java statements which are appropriate to the result of its conditional test.

The program below assigns an appropriate value to a String variable after determining if a tested number is odd or even:

Conditional.java

Notice here how the result variable is reused efficiently.

```java
public class Conditional
{
  public static void main (String[] args)
  {
    int num1 = 1357, num2 = 2468;   // numbers to test
    String result;       // variable for result strings

    // test first number & assign string
    result = ( num1 % 2 != 0 ) ? "Odd" : "Even";
    System.out.println( num1 + " is "+result );

    // test second number and assign string
    result = ( num2 % 2 != 0 ) ? "Odd" : "Even";
    System.out.println( num2 + " is "+result );
  }
}
```

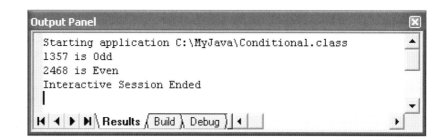

```
Output Panel                                          ☒

  Starting application C:\MyJava\Conditional.class
  1357 is Odd
  2468 is Even
  Interactive Session Ended
  |

 |◀ ◀ ▶ ▶| \ Results ⟨ Build ⟩ Debug ⟩ | ◀ |
```

Making statements

Statements are used in Java to progress the execution of a program. They may define loops within the code or be expressions to be evaluated. This chapter examines conditional testing and illustrates different types of loops.

Covers

Chapter Three

Conditional if

The "if" keyword is used to perform the basic conditional Java test to evaluate an expression for a boolean value. Any statement following the evaluation will only be executed when the expression returns true.

The syntax for the "if" statement looks like this:

```
if ( test-expression ) code-to-be-executed-when-true ;
```

The code to be executed may contain multiple statements if they are enclosed within a pair of curly brackets to form a "statement block".

In the program below, the test expression evaluates whether one number is greater than another.

If the first number is, in fact, greater than the second number the expression will be true and the code following the test will be executed.

If the expression was false the code following the test would not be executed and the program would just move along to the next statement.

IfDemo.java

The test expression could alternatively use if(1<5).

```java
public class IfDemo
{
   public static void main (String[] args)
   {
      if( 5>1 ) System.out.println("5 is greater than 1");
      System.out.println("Thanks for asking");
   }
}
```

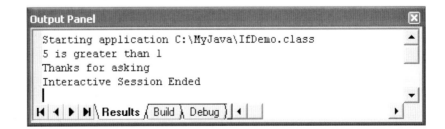

```
Output Panel                                            [X]
 Starting application C:\MyJava\IfDemo.class        ▲
 5 is greater than 1
 Thanks for asking
 Interactive Session Ended
 |                                                   ▼
 |◄ ◄ ► ►|\ Results / Build \ Debug }|◄|  |          ►
```

There are a number of ways to state an expression so that it may be tested for a boolean value of true:

Is the statement true?
The simplest expression evaluates a single statement to see if it is true or false and has this syntax:

```
if ( condition == true ) execute-this-code ;
```

The tests use a "==" equality operator, not a "=" assignment operator.

If the evaluation returns true then the code will be executed, like the example on the facing page.

The test will automatically look for a true return so it can be written without the "==true" part of the syntax, like this:

```
if ( condition ) execute-this-code ;
```

When a condition is false, it is true that the condition is false.

Is the statement false?
The boolean NOT operator can be added to a test expression so that the evaluation will return true only when the expression itself is false:

```
if ( ! condition ) execute-this-code ;
```

Are both statements true?
The boolean AND operator can be added to a test expression so that the evaluation will return true only when both test statements are true:

```
if ( condition1 && condition2 ) execute-this-code ;
```

Is either statement true?
The boolean OR operator can be added to a test expression so that the evaluation will return true only when either test statement is true:

```
if ( condition1 || condition2 ) execute-this-code ;
```

A combination of these may also form a test expression.

If-else statements

The Java "else" keyword can be used with an "if" statement to provide alternative code to be executed in the event that the test expression returns false.

This is called "conditional branching" and has this syntax:

The semicolon is required after the first code statement before starting the "else" alternative code.

```
if ( test-expression ) do-this ; else do-this-instead ;
```

Several expressions may be tested until a true value is found when the code following the true expression is executed.

It is important to note that any further code contained in the "if-else" statement is ignored. So in the following program any code after second test is ignored:

ElseDemo.java

In this example !bool is code shorthand for bool==false.

```java
public class ElseDemo
{
  public static void main (String[] args)
  {
    int num = 2; boolean bool = false;

    if( num == 2 && bool )
      System.out.println("1 is Correct");
    else
    if( num == 2 && !bool )
      System.out.println("2 is Correct");
    else
    if( num == 2 && !bool )
      System.out.println("The expression is true but
                          you will never see this output");
  }
}
```

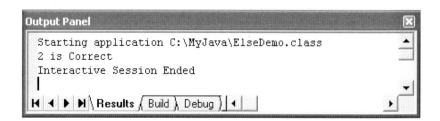

```
Output Panel                                          [X]
Starting application C:\MyJava\ElseDemo.class
2 is Correct
Interactive Session Ended
|
|◄ ◄ ► ►|\ Results / Build \ Debug ]| ◄ |        ►
```

The switch statement

Conditional branching using an "if-else" statement may be more efficiently performed using a "switch" statement when the test expression just evaluates a single integer value.

The switch statement works in an unusual way. It takes a given integer value then seeks a matching value among a number of "case" statements.

Code associated with the matching case statement will be executed or "default" code may execute if no match is found.

Each case statement must end with a "break" statement to prevent the program continuing through the switch block.

This program executes the appropriate case statement code then moves on to the next statement after the switch block:

SwitchDemo.java

This program could have been written using "if-else" statements like if(num==1)...; else if(num==2)...; etc.

```java
public class SwitchDemo
{
  public static void main (String[] args)
  {
    int num = 2;
    switch(num)
    {
      case 1 : System.out.println("Number is 1"); break;
      case 2 : System.out.println("Number is 2"); break;
      case 3 : System.out.println("Number is 3"); break;
      default: System.out.println("Other number");
    }
    System.out.println("Program Ends");
  }
}
```

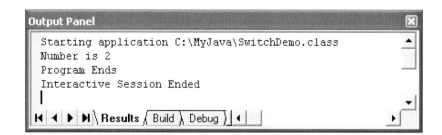

Output Panel

```
Starting application C:\MyJava\SwitchDemo.class
Number is 2
Program Ends
Interactive Session Ended
```

Results Build Debug

For loops

The "for" loop is probably the most frequently used type of loop in Java and has this syntax:

```
for( initializer ; test ; increment } { code-to-execute }
```

The initializer is used to set the start value for the counter of the number of loop iterations. A variable may be declared here for this purpose and it is traditional to name it "i".

At each pass of the loop a boolean condition is tested and the next iteration of the loop will run if the test returns true.
The loop will end when the tested expression returns false.

With every iteration the counter is incremented, then the loop will execute the code in the statement block.

This program contains a loop that makes three iterations and increments the value of two variables at each pass:

ForLoop.java

A "for" loop can count down by using i-- to decrement the counter.

```java
public class ForLoop
{
  public static void main(String[] args)
  {
    int a = 0, b = 0;
    for(int i = 0; i < 3; i++)
    {
      a += 10; b += 5;
      System.out.println("A is "+a+"  B is "+b);
    }
  }
}
```

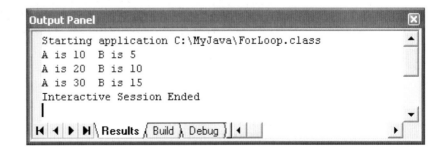

```
Output Panel                                            ☒
  Starting application C:\MyJava\ForLoop.class      ▲
  A is 10   B is 5
  A is 20   B is 10
  A is 30   B is 15
  Interactive Session Ended
  |                                                 ▼
 ⏮ ◀ ▶ ⏭ \ Results ⟨ Build ⟩⟨ Debug ⟩ ◀          ▶
```

While loops

Another type of loop uses the Java "while" keyword followed by an expression to be evaluated for a boolean value.

If the evaluation returns true then the code in the statement block will be executed. After the code has executed, the test expression will again be evaluated and the loop will continue until the evaluation returns false.

An infinite loop will lock the program as it continues to run iterations.

The statement block must feature code that will affect the test expression in order to change the evaluation result to return false, otherwise an infinite loop will be created.

Note that if the test expression returns false when it is first evaluated the code in the statement block is never executed.

This program decrements two variable values on each iteration and decrements the counter until it reaches zero when the evaluation returns false and the loop ends.

WhileLoop.java

```java
public class WhileLoop
{
  public static void main(String[] args)
  {
    int a = 30, b = 15, i = 3;
    while (i > 0)
    {
      a -= 10; b -= 5; i--;
      System.out.println("A is "+a+"  B is "+b);
    }
  }
}
```

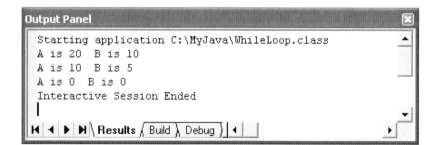

```
Output Panel                                              ☒
  Starting application C:\MyJava\WhileLoop.class        ▲
  A is 20  B is 10
  A is 10  B is 5
  A is 0  B is 0
  Interactive Session Ended
  |                                                      ▼
  ◄ ◄ ► ►| \ Results ⟨ Build ⟩ Debug ⟩ | ◄              ►
```

The do-while loop

The Java "do" keyword is used at the start of a "do-while" loop and is followed by a statement block containing the code to be executed by the loop.

The statement code is followed by the Java "while" keyword and a test expression to be evaluated for a boolean value.

If the evaluation returns true the loop restarts at the "do" keyword and will continue until the evaluation returns false.

It is important to note that, unlike the simple "while" loop, the statement code will always be executed at least once by the "do-while" loop because the test expression is not encountered until the end of the loop.

The following program will never loop because the counter value is incremented to 1 in the first execution of the statement code so the first test evaluation will return false:

DoWhile.java

A "while" loop is often more suitable than a "do-while" loop.

```java
public class DoWhile
{
  public static void main(String[] args)
  {
    int a = 0, i = 0;
    do
    {
      ++a;
      ++i;
      System.out.println("A is "+a);
    }
    while(i < 1);
  }
}
```

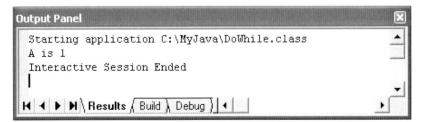

```
Output Panel                                        [x]

  Starting application C:\MyJava\DoWhile.class
  A is 1
  Interactive Session Ended
  |

  |◄ ◄ ► ►|\ Results / Build \ Debug }| ◄ |        ►
```

Break statement

The Java "break" keyword is used to terminate the execution of a loop prematurely.

The "break" statement is situated inside the statement block containing the code that the loop should execute and is preceded by a conditional test.

When the test condition is met the "break" statement immediately terminates the loop and no further iterations are made.

Notice in the program output below that the counter value is still 3 – because the increment in the final iteration is not applied.

In this program the loop would normally make five passes.

Because the conditional test returns true when the counter value reaches three, the break statement will exit the loop:

BreakDemo.java

The "break" keyword is also used as a terminator with the "switch" statement.

```java
public class BreakDemo
{
  public static void main(String[] args)
  {
    int i = 0;
    while ( i < 6 )
    {
      if (i == 3) break;
      i++;
    }
    System.out.println("Loop stopped at "+i);
  }
}
```

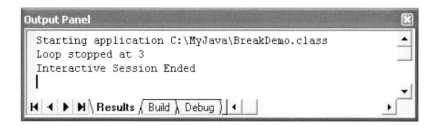

Output Panel

```
Starting application C:\MyJava\BreakDemo.class
Loop stopped at 3
Interactive Session Ended
```

Results / Build / Debug

Continue statement

The Java "continue" keyword is used to break the current iteration of a loop.

Just like a "break" statement, the "continue" statement is situated inside the statement block containing the code that the loop should execute, preceded by a conditional test.

When the test condition is met the continue statement immediately stops the current iteration of the loop but further iterations will be made until the loop ends.

The loop counter must be incremented before the "continue" condition is tested to avoid creating an infinite loop.

In the program below the test condition is met when the counter value reaches 3. So that iteration is skipped but the loop continues to complete the later iterations.

ContDemo.java

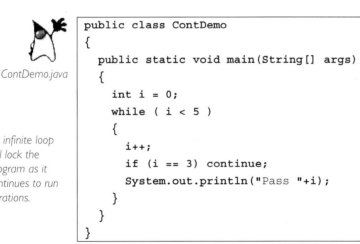

```java
public class ContDemo
{
  public static void main(String[] args)
  {
    int i = 0;
    while ( i < 5 )
    {
      i++;
      if (i == 3) continue;
      System.out.println("Pass "+i);
    }
  }
}
```

An infinite loop will lock the program as it continues to run iterations.

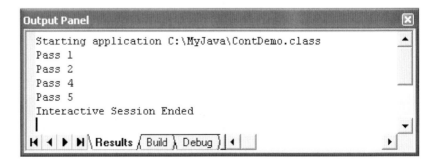

```
Output Panel                                         ☒
  Starting application C:\MyJava\ContDemo.class    ▲
  Pass 1
  Pass 2
  Pass 4
  Pass 5
  Interactive Session Ended
  |                                                 ▼
 ◄ ◄ ► ►\ Results ⟨ Build ⟩ Debug ⟩ ◄           ►
```

Adding labels

A loop may be nested to run inside an outer loop.

Using "break" or "continue" statements with nested loops can be better controlled by adding a label to the code to specify the point at which the program should resume the loop.

In the program below during the second pass the inner loop halts on its second iteration and resumes at the label.

If the "continue" statement had not specified this label point the inner loop would have completed a third iteration.

LabelDemo.java

A "break" statement could be used to halt just the inner loop then resume the outer loop.

```java
public class LabelDemo
{
  public static void main(String[] args)
  {
    outerLoop:
    for (int i = 1 ; i < 4; i++)
    {
      for (int j = 1; j < 4; j++)
      {
        if(i == 2 && j == 2) continue outerLoop;
        System.out.println("I is "+i+"  J is "+j);
      }
    }
  }
}
```

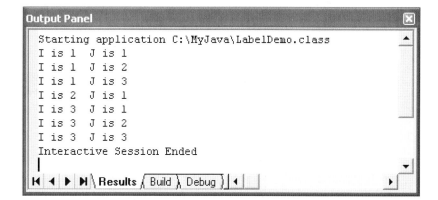

```
Output Panel                                           ☒
 Starting application C:\MyJava\LabelDemo.class        ▲
 I is 1  J is 1
 I is 1  J is 2
 I is 1  J is 3
 I is 2  J is 1
 I is 3  J is 1
 I is 3  J is 2
 I is 3  J is 3
 Interactive Session Ended
 |                                                     ▼
 ⏮ ◀ ▶ ⏭ \ Results ⟋ Build ⟍ Debug ⟋ | ◀ |      ▶
```

Return statement

The Java "return" keyword can be used to halt the execution of all further statements in the method.

When a "return" statement is encountered the program will return to a point that called the method or, if the program only contains one method, the program will end.

The program below contains a single method that includes a "return" statement inside a statement block.

When the condition is found to be true the statements in this block are executed and the method ends when the "return" statement is executed.

ReturnDemo.java

The "return" keyword can also be used to pass values at the conclusion of a method – see page 87.

```java
public class ReturnDemo
{
  public static void main(String[] args)
  {
    int i=1;
    System.out.println("Step "+i);
    i++;
    if(i==2)
    {
      System.out.println("Step "+i);
      System.out.println("Program Stopped");
      return;
    }
    System.out.println("This text will not be seen");
  }
}
```

Output Panel

```
Starting application C:\MyJava\ReturnDemo.class
Step 1
Step 2
Program Stopped
Interactive Session Ended
```

Results / Build \ Debug

Using arrays

This chapter deals exclusively with the topic of arrays and illustrates by example what they are and how to use them. The examples also demonstrate how array contents may be sorted into order.

Covers

Chapter Four

Creating arrays

An array is just a variable that can contain multiple values, unlike a regular variable that may only contain a single value.

An array declaration must first state its data type, with the usual data type keywords, but followed by square brackets to denote that it will be an array variable.

This, in turn, is followed by a given name for the array that adheres to the normal naming conventions.

Values of the correct data type can then be assigned to the array as a comma-delimited list enclosed in curly brackets.

The size of the array will be the length of the assigned list.

Stored values are indexed starting at zero and each value can be addressed by its index position in the list.

The program below first creates and initializes an array to store integers then outputs each of the stored values:

ArrayDemo.java

Remember that an array index starts at zero. So num[2] is the third element in an array, not the second.

```java
public class ArrayDemo
{
  public static void main(String[] args)
  {
   int[] num = {100, 200, 300};

   System.out.println("First stored value is "+num[0]);
   System.out.println("Second stored value is"+num[1]);
   System.out.println("Third stored value is "+num[2]);
  }
}
```

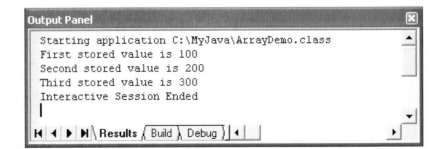

```
Output Panel                                              ☒
  Starting application C:\MyJava\ArrayDemo.class        ▲
  First stored value is 100
  Second stored value is 200
  Third stored value is 300
  Interactive Session Ended
  |                                                     ▼
 ⏮ ◀ ▶ ⏭ \ Results / Build \ Debug / ◀              ▶
```

Each value held in an array is called an array "element".

The total number of elements in an array is stored as an integer in the "length" property of that array. This can be useful in Java programming to report the size of the array.

The syntax to address an array's length property just tacks a period and "length" after the array's name.

So "myNums.length" references the length property of the array named "myNums".

Notice that an array containing three values will have a length of 3, but because indexing starts at zero the last element in the array will have an index number of only 2.

The program below creates a String array then reports its length and displays all the array elements' values:

Elems.java

Enclose String values in double quotes – and char values in single quotes.

```java
public class Elems
{
  public static void main(String[] args)
  {
   // create & initialize a String array
   String[] str = {"Much ", "More ", "Java"};

   // report the array length
   System.out.println("No. of elements is "+str.length);

   // concatenate & output all elements
   System.out.println(str[0] + str[1] + str[2]);
  }
}
```

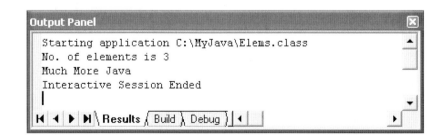

```
Output Panel                                              ☒
 Starting application C:\MyJava\Elems.class
 No. of elements is 3
 Much More Java
 Interactive Session Ended
|

|◄ ◄ ► ►|\ Results ╱ Build ╲ Debug ╲|◄ |                ►
```

Creating empty arrays

In order to create a new array without specifying any initial values the array declaration must assign a size for the array.

The assignment uses the Java "new" keyword to construct an empty array with the appropriate data type keyword.

An integer inside the square brackets following this data type keyword specifies the size of the empty array.

The elements are assigned default values of zero for **int** and **float** types, null for **String** types, \0 for **char** types, and false for **boolean** types.

The program below creates an **int** array then assigns values to just two elements. The values of all elements are output and the default value is displayed for the third element.

EmptyArray.java

If no other value is assigned to an array element the element will keep its default value.

```java
public class EmptyArray
{
  public static void main(String[] args)
  {
    // create an empty int array of 3 elements
    int[] num = new int[3];

    num[0] = 100; num[1] = 200;

    System.out.println("Index Zero is " + num[0]);
    System.out.println("Index One is " + num[1]);
    System.out.println("Index Two is " + num[2]);
  }
}
```

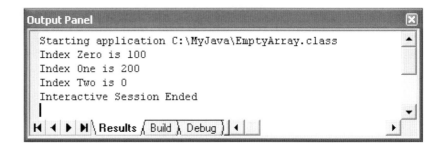

Output Panel

```
Starting application C:\MyJava\EmptyArray.class
Index Zero is 100
Index One is 200
Index Two is 0
Interactive Session Ended
```

Results / Build \ Debug

Read elements loop

All types of loop can be used to easily read all the values stored inside elements of an array.

The loop counter should start with the first index number then proceed on up to the final index number.

The last index number in an array will always be one less than the array length because the index starts at zero.

It is useful to set the array length property value as the conditional test determining when the loop should end.

The program below uses a for loop to iterate from the start element through to the final element in an array.

Each iteration outputs the value contained in the array element having the same index number as the counter value.

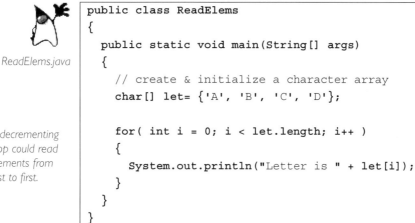

ReadElems.java

A decrementing loop could read elements from last to first.

```java
public class ReadElems
{
  public static void main(String[] args)
  {
    // create & initialize a character array
    char[] let= {'A', 'B', 'C', 'D'};

    for( int i = 0; i < let.length; i++ )
    {
      System.out.println("Letter is " + let[i]);
    }
  }
}
```

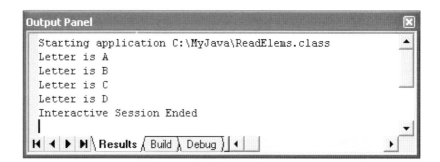

```
Output Panel                                          ☒
  Starting application C:\MyJava\ReadElems.class      ▲
  Letter is A
  Letter is B
  Letter is C
  Letter is D
  Interactive Session Ended
  |                                                   ▼
  ⏮ ◀ ▶ ⏭ \ Results ⟨ Build ⟨ Debug ⟩ ◀           ▶
```

Sorting array elements

The general features of Java are made available to all Java programs from the ready-made code in the **java.lang** class.

Further functionality can be made available to programs by also using other ready-made Java classes.

For instance, the **java.util** class provides a means to sort elements in a numerical array into their numeric order.

To add this functionality to a program requires simply that an import statement be added at the start of the program.

The "import" keyword should be followed by the required class name then a dot and the "★" wildcard character to ensure that all functions in that class are made available.

This program imports all functionality of the **java.util** class to make the **Arrays.sort()** method available:

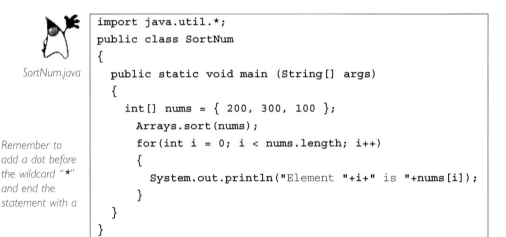

SortNum.java

```java
import java.util.*;
public class SortNum
{
  public static void main (String[] args)
  {
    int[] nums = { 200, 300, 100 };
    Arrays.sort(nums);
    for(int i = 0; i < nums.length; i++)
    {
      System.out.println("Element "+i+" is "+nums[i]);
    }
  }
}
```

Remember to add a dot before the wildcard "★" and end the statement with a semicolon.

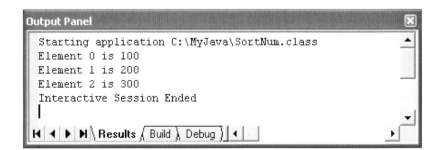

```
Output Panel                                              ☒
  Starting application C:\MyJava\SortNum.class          ▲
  Element 0 is 100
  Element 1 is 200
  Element 2 is 300
  Interactive Session Ended
  |                                                     ▼
|◀ ◀ ▶ ▶|\ Results / Build \ Debug |◀        ▶
```

The example on the facing page imports the capability to sort array elements from the **java.util** class library.

More precisely, it imports all the **java.util** functionality including the **sort()** method of the **Arrays** sub class.

The correct form of addressing a Java sub class is to append its name, after a dot, onto the parent class name.

So the **Arrays** sub class of the **java.util** class can correctly be addressed as **java.util.Arrays**.

When any Java sub class is imported into a program all of its methods become available to the program.

The program below explicitly imports the **java.util.Arrays** sub class to make its **sort()** method available so the program can arrange an array of string elements alphabetically:

SortNames.java

```
import java.util.Arrays;
public class SortNames
{
  public static void main (String[] args)
  {
    String[] names = { "Michael", "David", "Andrew" };
    Arrays.sort(names);
      for(int i = 0; i < names.length; i++)
    {
        System.out.println("Element "+i+" is "+names[i]);
    }
  }
}
```

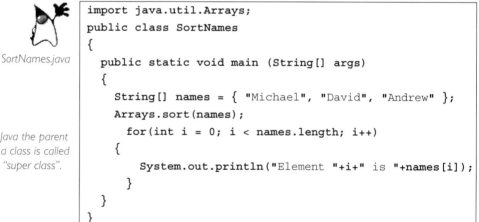

In Java the parent of a class is called its "super class".

HOT TIP

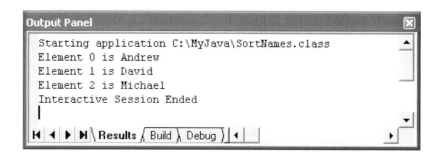

Output Panel ☒

```
Starting application C:\MyJava\SortNames.class
Element 0 is Andrew
Element 1 is David
Element 2 is Michael
Interactive Session Ended
|
```

⏮ ◀ ▶ ⏭ \ **Results** / Build \ Debug }| ◀ | ▶

Two-dimensional arrays

Arrays can be made to store two sets of element values by creating a two-dimensional array.

This "array of arrays" is simply created by declaring an array, as usual, followed by a second set of square brackets. Typically this is useful to store XY coordinates as references to specific points in a grid arrangement.

The program below uses a two-dimensional array to store the XY coordinates of three points in a grid 5 wide and 3 high:

Points.java

```java
public class Points
{
  public static void main(String[] args)
  {
      boolean[][] pts = new boolean[3][5];
      pts[0][2] = true;
      pts[1][1] = true;
      pts[2][4]= true;

      for(int i = 0; i < 3; i++)
      {
      for(int j = 0; j < 5; j++)
        {
          char mark = (pts[i][j] == true) ? 'X' : 'o';
             System.out.print(mark);
        }
        System.out.print("\n");
      }
  }
}
```

Three-dimensional arrays can be created by adding a third set of square brackets – but these can be difficult to comprehend.

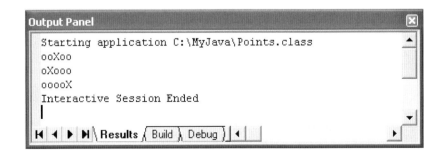

```
Output Panel                                          ☒
  Starting application C:\MyJava\Points.class
  ooXoo
  oXooo
  ooooX
  Interactive Session Ended
  |
  |◄ ◄ ► ►|\ Results / Build \ Debug / | ◄
```

Doing mathematics

This chapter introduces the **Java Math** class methods that can be used to perform mathematical calculations. Examples also illustrate formatting of numbers and currency plus the generation of random numbers.

Covers

Chapter Five

Math constants

The basic **java.lang** class that is available to all Java programs has a sub class called "Math" that contains features useful for performing mathematical calculations in Java programs.

The **Math** class contains two stored constant mathematical values that are often used in programs.

Math.PI stores the value of pi and **Math.E** stores the value of the base of natural logarithms.

Both of these are stored as double precision data types.

The program below displays both constant values then converts the **Math.PI** constant to a float data type to perform a calculation with another floating-point number:

ShowPi.java

```java
public class ShowPi
{
  public static void main(String[] args)
  {
      float radius = 5f;
      float pi = (float) Math.PI;
      float area= pi * (radius * radius);

      System.out.println("Pi constant is " + Math.PI);
      System.out.println("Pi float is " + pi);
      System.out.println("Circle radius is " + radius);
      System.out.println("Area of circle is " + area);
  }
}
```

The technique of converting one data type to another is called "casting".

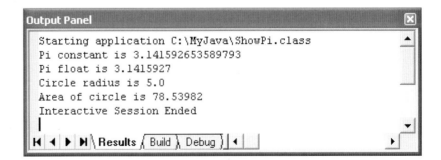

Output Panel

```
Starting application C:\MyJava\ShowPi.class
Pi constant is 3.141592653589793
Pi float is 3.1415927
Circle radius is 5.0
Area of circle is 78.53982
Interactive Session Ended

|
```

H ◀ ▶ H \ Results / Build \ Debug] | ◀

Math methods

The table below lists the **java.lang.Math** methods that can be used to perform mathematical calculations.

Most of the Math methods will return a double data type result.

Method	Returns
abs()	Absolute value of a number
acos()	Arc cosine of an angle
asin()	Arc sine of an angle
atan()	Arc tangent of an angle
atan2()	Rectangular coordinates converted to polar
ceil()	Smallest value equal to an integer
cos()	Trigonometric cosine of an angle
exp()	Math.E to the power of a number
floor()	Largest value equal to an integer
log()	Natural logarithm of a number
max()	Greater of two numbers
min()	Smaller of two numbers
pow()	First argument to the power of the second
random()	Random positive value between 0.0 and 1.0
rint()	Closest number equal to an integer
round()	Closest integer
sin()	Trigonometric sine of an angle
sqrt()	Square root of a number
tan()	Trigonometric tangent of an angle
toDegrees()	Angle in degrees from angle in radians
toRadians()	Angle in radians from angle in degrees

Comparing numbers

Math methods require a given number, or numbers, to be stated as arguments in the brackets following their name.

The **Math.min()** and **Math.max()** methods require two given numbers to be stated as arguments for comparison.

Math.min() will return the smallest of the two given numbers while **Math.max()** will return the greater number.

Both methods return results as double data type numbers.

The following program uses both int and float data type numbers for comparison by these methods and the results are output as double precision floating-point numbers.

Finally the returned max double data type is cast to an int data type variable that is output as an integer number.

Compare.java

```java
public class Compare
{
  public static void main(String[] args)
  {
    int num1 = 25;
    float num2 = 24.75f;

    System.out.println("Least is "+Math.min(num1,num2));
    System.out.println("Most is "+Math.max(num1,num2));

    int conv = (int) Math.max(num1,num2);
    System.out.println("Converted double is "+conv);
  }
}
```

To cast data types prefix the value by brackets containing the data type to which it should be converted.

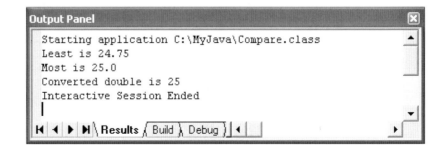

Output Panel

```
Starting application C:\MyJava\Compare.class
Least is 24.75
Most is 25.0
Converted double is 25
Interactive Session Ended
```

H ◀ ▶ H \ Results / Build \ Debug \ ◀

Rounding floating-point numbers

The **Math** class provides three ways to round floating-point numbers to the nearest integer numbers.

Simplest of these is the **Math.round()** method that rounds a given number up or down to the closest integer.

Math.round() returns its result as an **int** data type.

Alternatively the **Math.floor()** method rounds down to the closest integer below a given number while the **Math.ceil()** method will round up to the closest integer above it.

Math.floor() and **Math.ceil()** return double data type results.

In the program below **Math.round()** returns an **int** data type that is the closest integer to the **num** variable.

Math.floor() and **Math.ceil()** return double data type numbers that are equal to the closest integer below and above the **num** variable value.

Round.java

By default **Math.round()** *will round up – so 7.5 would be rounded to 8.*

```
public class Round
{
  public static void main(String[] args)
  {
    float num = 7.25f;

      System.out.println("Rounded is "+ Math.round(num));
      System.out.println("Floored is "+ Math.floor(num));
      System.out.println("Ceiling is "+ Math.ceil(num));
  }
}
```

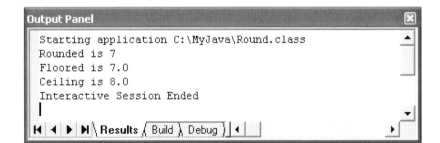

```
Output Panel                                              ☒
    Starting application C:\MyJava\Round.class
    Rounded is 7
    Floored is 7.0
    Ceiling is 8.0
    Interactive Session Ended

  ⏮ ◀ ▶ ⏭ \ Results ⟨ Build ⟩ Debug ⟩⟨ ◀ │
```

Random number generator

Random numbers can be generated using the **Math.random()** method to return a double type number between 0.0 and 1.0.

Multiplying the random number will specify a wider range so, for example, a multiplier of 10 will create a random number that is now between 0.0 and 10.0.

The **Math.ceil()** method can be used to round numbers up – so in this case the range becomes between 1 and 10 inclusive.

This program demonstrates each of these stages then creates another rounded random integer by combining all stages:

Random.java

```
public class Random
{
 public static void main(String[] args)
 {
   float rand1 = (float) Math.random();
   float rand2 = rand1 * 10;
   int rand3 = (int)Math.ceil(rand2);

   System.out.println("Basic random is "+rand1);
   System.out.println("Bigger range random is "+rand2);
   System.out.println("Rounded up random is "+rand3);

   // create a random integer between 1 and 10 inclusive
   int r = (int) Math.ceil( Math.random() * 10 );
   System.out.println("Another rounded random is "+r);   }
}
```

Math.random() can create a series of selections, like a lottery draw.

Output Panel ☒

```
 Starting application C:\MyJava\Random.class
 Basic random is 0.54166806
 Bigger range random is 5.4166803
 Rounded up random is 6
 Another rounded random is 3
 Interactive Session Ended
 |
```

⊪ ◀ ▶ ▶⊩ \ Results ⟨ Build ⟩ Debug ⟩| ◀ |

This program uses **Math.random()** to generate a series of six random numbers within a range of 1 to 49 which can be used as selections in a lottery using numbers of that range.

Lottery.java

```
public class Lottery
{
  public static void main(String[] args)
  {
   int[] a = {0,0,0,0,0,0};

   while(a[5]== 0)
   {
    int n = (int) Math.ceil(Math.random() * 49 );

    if(a[0] == 0) a[0] = n;
    else if(a[1] == 0 && n != a[0])     a[1] = n;
    else if(a[2] == 0 && n != a[0] && n !=a [1])a[2] = n;
    else if(a[3] == 0 && n != a[0] && n != a[1]
                               && n!=a[2])a[3] = n;
    else if(a[4] == 0 && n != a[0] && n != a[1]
             && n != a[2] && n != a[3]) a[4] = n;
    else if(a[5] == 0 && n != a[0] && n != a[1]
       && n != a[2] && n != a[3] && n != a[5]) a[5] = n;
   }

   System.out.print("LUCKY NUMBERS: ");
   for(int i = 0; i < 6; i++)
   {
     System.out.print(a[i]+" ");
   }
  }
}
```

The random numbers are placed into the "a" array only if they have not been previously selected.

Output Panel

```
Starting application C:\MyJava\Lottery.class
LUCKY NUMBERS: 7 33 49 17 34 26
Interactive Session Ended
```

Results / Build \ Debug

Formatting numbers and currencies

Output numbers from a Java program can be made more easily readable with the formatting options provided in the **java.text** class.

To make these options available to the program an import statement must be included at the start of the code.

This allows NumberFormat objects to be created, in a similar way to that for regular variables, but they may be used to format plain numbers, currency or percentages.

Each NumberFormat object has a **format()** method that accepts the number to be formatted as its single argument.

The program below creates a NumberFormat object for each of the three formatting options then uses the **format()** method of each object to format its given number:

NumFormat.java

The formatted output is a String data type – not a number.

```java
import java.text.*;

public class NumFormat
{
  public static void main(String[] args)
  {
   NumberFormat nf = NumberFormat.getNumberInstance();
   NumberFormat cf = NumberFormat.getCurrencyInstance();
   NumberFormat pf = NumberFormat.getPercentInstance();
   System.out.println(nf.format(123456789.00f));
   System.out.println(cf.format(1234.50f));
   System.out.println(pf.format(0.75f));
  }
}
```

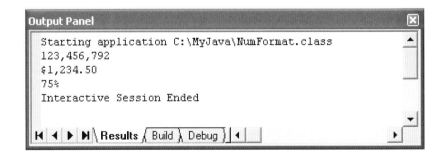

```
Output Panel                                            ☒
   Starting application C:\MyJava\NumFormat.class        ▲
   123,456,792
   $1,234.50
   75%
   Interactive Session Ended
                                                         ▼
 ⊮ ◄ ► ⊯ \ Results / Build \ Debug } ◄          ►
```

…cont'd

The formatted currency on the facing page uses the default currency of the local system setting in the USA but formats for other currencies are possible by specifying other locales.

The **java.util** class provides a way to specify other locales so an import statement needs to be added to import that class.

Locale objects are created with the new keyword and state the locale language and country as arguments given as their standard ISO two-letter abbreviations.

This program creates three locales to specify as the argument in **getCurrencyInstance()** to format three currency outputs:

CurrFormat.java

A list of all ISO abbreviations is widely available on the web – search for "ISO country codes" and "ISO language codes".

```java
import java.text.*; import java.util.*;

public class CurrFormat
{
  public static void main(String[] args)
  {
    Locale fra = new Locale("fr","FR"); // France
    Locale ger = new Locale("de","DE"); // Germany
      Locale uk = new Locale("en","GB"); // Great Britain
      NumberFormat num;
    num = NumberFormat.getCurrencyInstance(fra);
    System.out.println("Cash is "+num.format(2500.00f));
    num = NumberFormat.getCurrencyInstance(ger);
    System.out.println("Cash is "+num.format(2500.00f));
    num = NumberFormat.getCurrencyInstance(uk);
    System.out.println("Cash is "+num.format(2500.00f));
  }
}
```

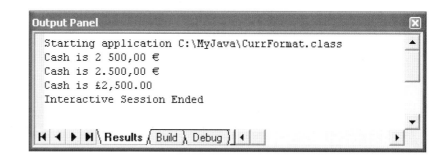

```
Output Panel
Starting application C:\MyJava\CurrFormat.class
Cash is 2 500,00 €
Cash is 2.500,00 €
Cash is £2,500.00
Interactive Session Ended
Results  Build  Debug
```

Numeric powers

The Java **Math.pow()** method is used to raise a given number to a specified power.

A given number is stated as the first argument to this method and a given power is stated as its second argument.

The method returns a double type number that is the value of the first argument raised to the power of the second.

Also the **Math.sqrt()** method can be used to return the square root of a number that is specified as its argument.

In the program below **Math.pow()** is used to create both the square and cube values of a given number then the **Math.sqrt()** method returns its square root value:

Power.java

The returned double values are cast to int values with the (int) code.

```java
public class Power
{
  public static void main(String[] args)
  {
    int num = 9;
    int square = (int) Math.pow(num, 2);
     int cube   = (int) Math.pow(num, 3);
    int sqRoot = (int) Math.sqrt(num);
    System.out.println("Number is " + num);
    System.out.println("Squared is " + square);
      System.out.println("Cubed is " + cube);
      System.out.println("Square Root is " + sqRoot);
  }
}
```

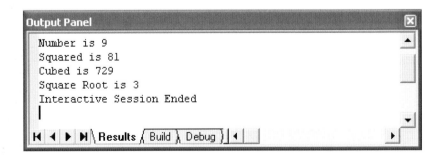

```
Output Panel                                          ☒
 Number is 9
 Squared is 81
 Cubed is 729
 Square Root is 3
 Interactive Session Ended
 |
 |◀ ◀ ▶ ▶|  Results ⟋ Build ⟍ Debug ⟍ ◀
```

Managing strings

This chapter illustrates how text strings can be manipulated and demonstrates by example how data can be passed to Java programs at run time.

Covers

Chapter Six

String length

A string in Java is simply zero or more characters enclosed within quotes – so these are all strings:

```
String str1 = "My First String";

String str2 = "";

String str3 = "2";

String str4 = "null";
```

The empty quotes in "str2" initialize the variable as an empty string value. The numeric value assigned to "str3" is a string representation of a number and the Java "null" keyword is just a string literal when enclosed by quotes.

Array.length is a property but *String.length()* is a method that needs to have following brackets.

Essentially a string is a collection of characters, each character containing its own data, just like elements in a defined array.

It is logical to regard a string as an array of characters and apply array characteristics when using strings.

The example below parallels the **array.length** property with the **String.length()** method to return the string's length:

StrLength.java

```java
public class StrLength
{
  public static void main(String[] args)
  {
    String str = "Java String";
    System.out.println(str+" is "+str.length()+" long");
  }
}
```

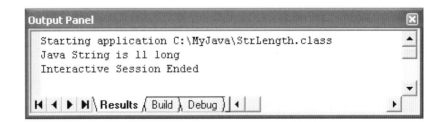

```
Output Panel                                              ✕
  Starting application C:\MyJava\StrLength.class
  Java String is 11 long
  Interactive Session Ended

  |◀ ◀ ▶ ▶|  Results ⟋ Build ⟍ Debug ⟍ ◀|        ▶
```

Joining strings

The "+" operator is used to concatenate strings and is widely used in the example code given throughout this book.

Also the **String.concat()** method can be used to concatenate strings and takes as its argument the string to be appended.

The program shown below uses both the "+" operator and the **String.concat()** method to join together several strings:

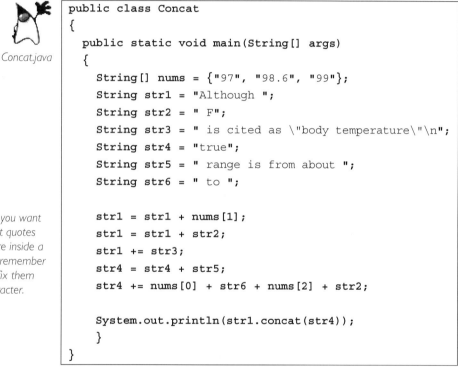

Concat.java

```java
public class Concat
{
  public static void main(String[] args)
  {
    String[] nums = {"97", "98.6", "99"};
    String str1 = "Although ";
    String str2 = " F";
    String str3 = " is cited as \"body temperature\"\n";
    String str4 = "true";
    String str5 = " range is from about ";
    String str6 = " to ";

    str1 = str1 + nums[1];
    str1 = str1 + str2;
    str1 += str3;
    str4 = str4 + str5;
    str4 += nums[0] + str6 + nums[2] + str2;

    System.out.println(str1.concat(str4));
  }
}
```

When you want to print quotes that are inside a string, remember to prefix them with a backslash character.

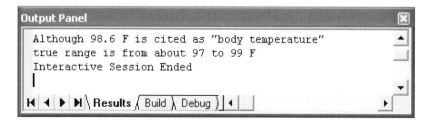

```
Output Panel                                                    ☒
  Although 98.6 F is cited as "body temperature"          ▲
  true range is from about 97 to 99 F
  Interactive Session Ended
  |                                                        ▼
  ◄◄ ◄ ► ►► \ Results / Build \ Debug / ◄        ►
```

Search a string

Java can search a string to find a character or substring passed as the argument to the **String.indexOf()** method.

If a match is made the method returns the starting position of the first occurrence of the matched character or substring within the searched string.

In the event that no match is found the **String.indexOf()** method returns a value of -1.

This program uses the **String.indexOf()** method to seek a dot and @ character within an email address string to perform a simple format validation:

Search.java

```
public class Search
{
  public static void main(String[] args)
  {
   String str = "mailme@domain.com";
   int isAt = str.indexOf("@");
   int isDot= str.indexOf(".");

   if( (isAt != -1) && (isDot != -1))
   {
    System.out.println("Format is Valid");
    System.out.println("@ found at character "+isAt);
    System.out.println("Dot found at character "+isDot);
   }
   else System.out.println("Format is Invalid");
  }
}
```

An optional second integer argument may specify the position from which to start the search.

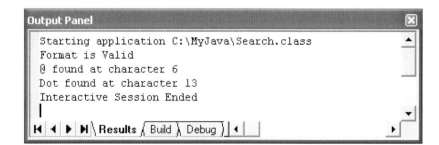

Output Panel

```
Starting application C:\MyJava\Search.class
Format is Valid
@ found at character 6
Dot found at character 13
Interactive Session Ended
|
```

H ◀ ▶ ▶H \ Results ⟨ Build ⟩ Debug ⟩ ◀

Substrings

A substring may be copied from an existing string using the **String.substring()** method.

This method takes a single argument to specify the starting position of the substring within the main string.

The returned string will be a substring of the main string from the character at the specified starting position up to the last character in the main string.

Optionally a second argument can be included to also state the end position of the substring within the main string.

The returned string will be a substring of the main string from the character at the specified starting position up to the character before the specified end position.

In the following program two substrings are copied into variables then displayed in concatenated output.

Substring.java

Notice how the output text mixes both String and int data types with the "+" operator.

```java
public class Substring
{
  public static void main(String[] args)
  {
    String str = "Java in easy steps";
    String sub1 = str.substring(0,5);
    String sub2 = str.substring(4);
    int num = 2;

    System.out.println("\n\t"+sub1+num+sub2+"\n");
  }
}
```

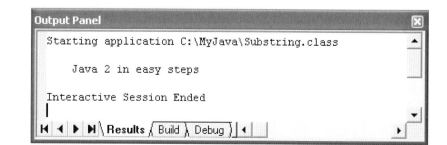

Comparing strings

The Java **String.startsWith()** and **String.endsWith()** methods can be useful to test string extremities against a comparison string passed as an argument to the method.

The program below tests the endings of a number of strings in an array and increments a counter when a match is found. It also tests the beginnings of the same strings and increments a second counter for successful matches.

CompEnds.java

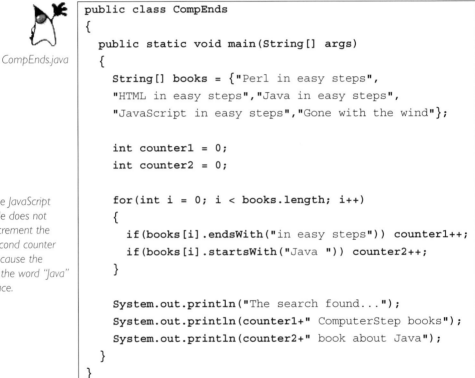

```java
public class CompEnds
{
  public static void main(String[] args)
  {
    String[] books = {"Perl in easy steps",
    "HTML in easy steps","Java in easy steps",
    "JavaScript in easy steps","Gone with the wind"};

    int counter1 = 0;
    int counter2 = 0;

    for(int i = 0; i < books.length; i++)
    {
      if(books[i].endsWith("in easy steps")) counter1++;
      if(books[i].startsWith("Java ")) counter2++;
    }

    System.out.println("The search found...");
    System.out.println(counter1+" ComputerStep books");
    System.out.println(counter2+" book about Java");
  }
}
```

The JavaScript title does not increment the second counter because the search is seeking the word "Java" followed by a space.

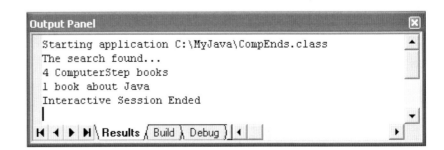

Output Panel

```
Starting application C:\MyJava\CompEnds.class
The search found...
4 ComputerStep books
1 book about Java
Interactive Session Ended
```

H ◄ ► H \ Results ⟨ Build ⟩ Debug ⟩ ◄

The equality operator "==" cannot be used to compare strings but the **String.equals()** method can be used instead.

This method takes a single argument that is the string to be tested against the original string.

When both strings have identical characters, and in the same order, the method returns a boolean true value.

If the strings are not identical in every respect the **String.equals()** method will return a boolean false value.

The program below first compares two different strings for equality and finds that they do not match.

Next the program compares a substring of the first string against the original string and finds that they exactly match.

Equal.java

Because Java is case-sensitive the character cases must also match for the method to return true.

```java
public class Equal
{
 public static void main(String[] args)
 {
   String str1 = "Personal Computer";
   String str2 = "Computer";
   String str3 = str1.substring(9);

   String result = str1.equals(str2)?"equal":"inequal";
   System.out.println(str1+" and "+str2 +" are "+result);

   result = str3.equals(str2) ? "equal" : "inequal";
   System.out.println(str3+" and "+str2 +" are "+result);
 }
}
```

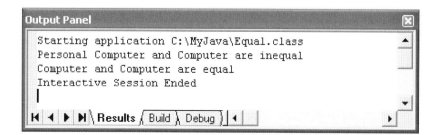

```
Output Panel                                              ☒
  Starting application C:\MyJava\Equal.class          ▲
  Personal Computer and Computer are inequal
  Computer and Computer are equal
  Interactive Session Ended
  |                                                     ▼
 |◄ ◄ ► ►|\ Results / Build \ Debug ]|◄ |        ►
```

Passing data to programs

The standard Java code that declares a main method includes an argument that creates a String array called "args".

The purpose of the **args[]** array is to allow data to be passed to the Java program when that program is called to run.

By convention the String array is named "args" but it could, in fact, bear any valid name.

Data to be passed to the program is added after a single space following the program name at the command line.

Multiple items of data can be passed to the program in this way and each item must be separated by a single space.

The program can then use the items of data that have been passed to it by referring to the elements of the **args[]** array.

The program below uses a common method to seek passed data items by checking the size of the **args[]** array. When elements are present the passed data is used in its output.

PassData.java

If a data item itself includes a space, surround the entire item with double quotes to pass it correctly.

```java
public class PassData
{
 public static void main(String[] args)
 {
  if(args.length > 0)
  {
   for(int i = 0; i < args.length; i++)
   {
    System.out.println("args["+i+"] is "+args[i]);
   }
  }
 }
}
```

```
C:\MyJava>java PassData Java is fun
args[0] is Java
args[1] is is
args[2] is fun
```

To pass data to programs in the JPadPro environment it is necessary to ensure that a preference option is selected to always display the "Run Java application" dialog box.

This option is found by clicking View on the toolbar then selecting the Preferences menu item.

In the Preferences dialog box tick the checkbox for the option "Always show choose application dialog".

Now whenever a program is called in JPadPro the Run dialog will offer the opportunity to pass data items to the program in a similar way to passing data from the command line.

Turn the option back off when not using this feature to prevent the Run dialog appearing every time a program is run.

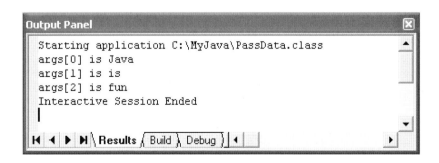

Converting strings

There are occasions when numeric values are stored in String data variables – such as when numbers are passed to the **args[]** array in a Java program.

The *Double* class also has a *parseDouble()* method and the *Byte* class has a *parseByte()* method.

In order for the program to use these numeric values they must first be converted into an appropriate data type.

All the numeric Java data types have corresponding classes containing methods that make these conversions simple.

The program below uses the **parseInt()** method of the **Integer** class, and the **parseFloat()** method of the **Float** class, to extract the numeric value from a String and assign it to an appropriate data type variable.

Convert.java

```
public class Convert
{
  public static void main(String[] args)
  {
    String str = "99";
    int num = Integer.parseInt(str);
    float dec = Float.parseFloat(str);

    str = Integer.toString(num);
    str = str.concat(" Red Balloons");

    System.out.println("int: "+num);
    System.out.println("float: "+dec);
    System.out.println("String: "+str);
  }
}
```

All numeric classes have a *toString()* method that converts number types to String types – like *Integer.toString()* seen here.

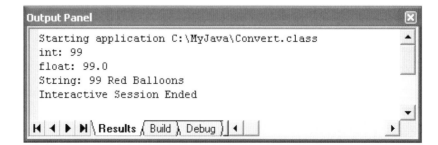

```
Output Panel                                              ☒

  Starting application C:\MyJava\Convert.class
  int: 99
  float: 99.0
  String: 99 Red Balloons
  Interactive Session Ended

  ⏮ ◀ ▶ ⏭ \ Results / Build \ Debug /| ◀        ▶
```

Changing case

The Java **String** class provides the **String.toUpperCase()** method to change string characters to uppercase, and the **String.toLowerCase()** method to change them to lowercase.

These methods are most useful before comparing two strings to ensure that both use the same character case.

A typical example might force a user input password string to lowercase characters before comparing it with the correct password stored as a string with only lowercase characters.

This would allow the user to input their password in uppercase, lowercase, or a mixture of both character cases, where case-insensitive passwords are permissible.

In the following program "BINGO", "bingo" and "BingO" would all be valid passwords:

Password.java

This example could equally have used the **toUpperCase()** *method to validate against "BINGO".*

```java
public class Password
{
  public static void main(String[] args)
  {
    if(args.length > 0)
    {
      String attempt = args[0];
      attempt = attempt.toLowerCase();
      if(attempt.equals("bingo"))
        System.out.println("Password is validated");
      else
        System.out.println("Sorry - Password Invalid");
    }
    else System.out.println("Please Enter Password");
  }
}
```

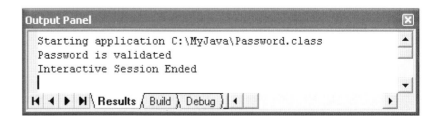

Output Panel

```
Starting application C:\MyJava\Password.class
Password is validated
Interactive Session Ended
```

◄ ◄ ► ►\ Results / Build \ Debug \ ◄

Replace letters and spaces

The **String.trim()** method removes any whitespace from the beginning and end of a string, including tabs and new lines.

All occurrences of a given character in a string may be replaced by another using the **String.replace()** method. This method takes two arguments to specify the character to be replaced and the new character that is to take its place.

String characters can be individually addressed using their index position as the argument to a **String.charAt()** method.

The following program demonstrates each of these in action:

Replace.java

```java
public class Replace
{
  public static void main(String[] args)
  {
    String str = "                Borrocudo    ";
      System.out.println("Original String: "+str);

    str = str.trim();
    System.out.println("Trimmed: "+str);

    char let = str.charAt(0);
    System.out.println("First Letter: "+let);

    str = str.replace('o','a');
    System.out.println("Replaced Character: "+str);
  }
}
```

Strings are like arrays of characters so their element index value is used as the argument in the String.charAt() method.

Output Panel ☒

```
Starting application C:\MyJava\Replace.class
Original String:
                    Borrocudo
Trimmed: Borrocudo
First Letter: B
Replaced Character: Barracuda
Interactive Session Ended
|
```

⏮ ◀ ▶ ⏭ \ Results ⟨ Build ⟩ Debug ⟩ ◀   ▶

Methods and classes

This chapter introduces programs with multiple methods and multiple classes. Examples illustrate how to pass values between methods, and the static and void declaration modifiers are explained.

Covers

Chapter Seven

Multiple methods

Normally programs are split into separate methods in order to create modules of code which each perform tasks and that can be called repeatedly throughout the program as required.

Splitting the program like this also makes it easier to find bugs as each method can be tested individually.

Further methods may be declared, inside the curly brackets that contain the class code, using the same keywords that are used to declare the main method.

The new method must be given a name, following the usual naming conventions, and may optionally specify arguments in the brackets after its name.

In this program a second method named "sub" is declared without any arguments. When the program runs the main method is called by the Java interpreter which, in turn, calls the sub method to execute the code in its statement block.

MultiMethod.java

To call another method just use its name followed by plain brackets.

```
public class MultiMethod
{
  public static void main(String[] args)
  {
    System.out.println("Message from the main method");
    sub();
  }

  public static void sub()
  {
    System.out.println("Message from the sub method");
  }
}
```

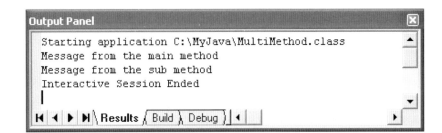

Output Panel

```
Starting application C:\MyJava\MultiMethod.class
Message from the main method
Message from the sub method
Interactive Session Ended
```

H ◀ ▶ H \ Results ╱ Build ╲ Debug ╱ ◀

Class variables and class methods

A "static" keyword creates "class variables" and "class methods" that are readily accessible throughout the class.

The main method is always declared as static. Static methods can only access other static methods.

So to be useful all other methods in a class must also be declared as static methods.

This example illustrates a class variable being used by the main method and another class method:

Scope.java

```
public class Scope
{
  static int number = 100;  // global class variable
  public static void main(String[] args)
  {
    int num = 250;  // local method variable
    System.out.println("Global Number is "+number);
    System.out.println("Main Number is "+num);
    sub();
  }

  public static void sub()
  {
    int num = 500;  // local method variable
    System.out.println("Global Number is "+number);
    System.out.println("Sub Number is "+num);
  }
}
```

The num variables have only local "scope" – with accessibility only inside the method where they are declared. This means they can have the same name without conflict.

Output Panel ☒

```
Starting application C:\MyJava\Scope.class
Global Number is 100
Main Number is 250
Global Number is 100
Sub Number is 500
Interactive Session Ended
|
```

⏮ ◀ ▶ ⏭ \ Results / Build \ Debug } ◀

Pass value to method

Methods in a program are generally more useful if values can be passed to them from other parts of the program.

The type of value that a method can accept is specified as an argument in the method's declaration and is given a name by which the method can refer to the passed value.

Multiple arguments can be specified, of the same or different data types, by separating them with a comma.

An appropriate value can then be passed as an argument when the method is called, either as a direct value of the expected type or as a variable of the expected type.

Calls to methods must state exactly the correct type and number of arguments that the method expects.

In this program the sub method will accept a String value that the method can refer to by the name "hat":

PassValue.java

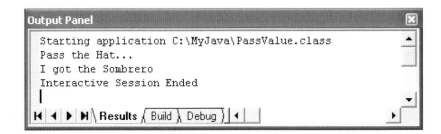

A passed value can be assigned to a variable for use like any other variable.

```java
public class PassValue
{
  public static void main(String[] args)
  {
    System.out.println("Pass the Hat...");
    sub("Sombrero");
  }

  public static void sub(String hat)
  {
    System.out.println("I got the " + hat);
  }
}
```

Output Panel ⊠

```
Starting application C:\MyJava\PassValue.class
Pass the Hat...
I got the Sombrero
Interactive Session Ended
```

H ◄ ► H \ Results ⟨ Build ⟩ Debug ⟩| ◄ |

Return value from method

A method can be allowed to return a value after it is called by stating the permissible return data type in its declaration in place of the "void" keyword that signifies no return.

The Java "return" keyword can then be used in the method's statement block to return an appropriate value to the caller.

A method that returns a value can be used in place of a variable or value anywhere in a program.

This example calls two methods that return values:

ReturnValue.java

```java
public class ReturnValue
{
  public static void main(String[] args)
  {
    int number = 25;
    System.out.println(number+" is "+ sub(number) );

    if( sub2(number) )
    System.out.println(number+" is above 10");
  }

  public static String sub(int num)
  {
    return (num % 2 == 0) ? "even" : "odd";
  }

  public static boolean sub2(int num)
  {
    return (num > 10) ? true : false;
  }
}
```

The declaration may specify any of the Java data types as the value to be returned by the method.

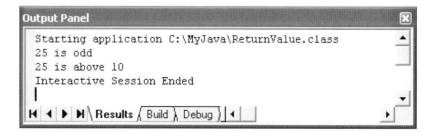

Output Panel

```
Starting application C:\MyJava\ReturnValue.class
25 is odd
25 is above 10
Interactive Session Ended
```

⏮ ◀ ▶ ⏭ \ Results / Build \ Debug) | ◀

Extend another class

Typically real-life programs are split into separate classes, in a similar way that classes can be split into separate methods.

The program still runs from the main method of the initial program class but the class declaration can add the "extends" keyword to include another class in a separate file.

Methods and variables in the included class can now be treated as though they existed in the main class file.

The first class containing the main method is termed the "super class" and the second class is termed the "sub class" to describe the relationship between the two classes.

When this program runs it outputs the line from its main method then calls the sub method in the **SubClass** class:

SuperClass.java

```java
public class SuperClass extends SubClass
{
  public static void main(String[] args)
  {
    System.out.println("Hello from the Super Class");
    sub();
  }
}
```

SubClass.class

```java
public class SubClass
{
  public static void sub()
  {
    System.out.println("Hello from the Sub Class");
  }
}
```

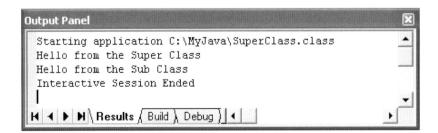

```
Output Panel                                              ⊠
  Starting application C:\MyJava\SuperClass.class        ▲
  Hello from the Super Class
  Hello from the Sub Class
  Interactive Session Ended
  |                                                       ▼
 ⏮ ◀ ▶ ⏭ \ Results / Build \ Debug } | ◀         ▶
```

Add another class

Classes can be added to an original file containing the class bearing the main method if they are declared without the "public" keyword access modifier.

This gives the class a default access status that is useful to define methods and properties for use in the program.

The program can address these features by prefixing their given name with their class name followed by a period.

In the example below another class is defined at the start of the program that contains a method and a variable which are used by the main method of the program's main class.

MainClass.java

```
class AnotherClass
{
  static String str = "Useful to Define Objects";
  public static void greeting()
  {
    System.out.println("Hello from the Another Class");
  }
}

public class MainClass
{
  public static void main(String[] args)
  {
    System.out.println("Hello from the Main Class");
    AnotherClass.greeting();
    System.out.println(AnotherClass.str);
  }
}
```

The syntax to use other class methods should look familiar – the code to output text addresses the "println()" method of the "out" sub class of the Java "System" class.

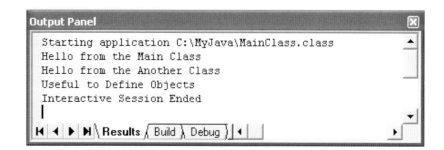

Output Panel   ☒

```
Starting application C:\MyJava\MainClass.class
Hello from the Main Class
Hello from the Another Class
Useful to Define Objects
Interactive Session Ended
|
```

⏮ ◀ ▶ ⏭ \ Results / Build \ Debug } | ◀ | ▶

Method overloading

A class may contain several methods bearing the same name if they each have different argument data types or require a different number of arguments to be passed.

This useful feature is called "method overloading" and is used in this program with three methods named "write":

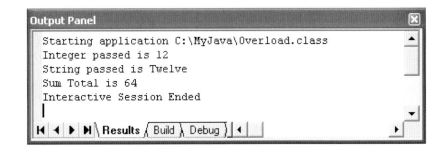

Overload.java

```java
public class Overload
{
  public static void main(String[] args)
  {
    System.out.println(write(12));
    System.out.println(write("Twelve"));
    System.out.println(write(4,16));
  }

  public static String write(String num)
  {
    return ("String passed is " + num);
  }

  public static String write(int num)
  {
    return ("Integer passed is " + num);
  }

  public static String write(int num, int another)
  {
    return ("Sum Total is "+(num * another) );
  }
}
```

Only use this technique for methods that have a related purpose – otherwise use different method names as usual.

Output Panel ☒

```
Starting application C:\MyJava\Overload.class
Integer passed is 12
String passed is Twelve
Sum Total is 64
Interactive Session Ended
```

|◄ ◄ ► ►|\ Results / Build \ Debug |◄

Programming with objects

This chapter introduces objects into Java programming. It defines what an object is and how to create an object in a program. Examples illustrate how to create new instances of an object and how to use their methods and properties.

Covers

Chapter Eight

What is an object?

Real world objects are all around us and they each have attributes and behaviors that we can describe.

Attributes describe features of an object and behaviors describe what an object actually does.

For instance, a car might be described with attributes of "red" and "coupe" along with an "accelerates" behavior.

These features could be represented in Java programming with a **Car** class containing variable properties of **color** and **body-type** along with an **accelerates()** method.

Java is said to be an "object-oriented" programming language because it makes extensive use of object attributes and behaviors to perform program tasks.

Objects are created in Java by defining a class as a template from which different copies, or "instances" can be made.

Each instance of the class can be customized by assigning attribute values and behaviors to describe that object.

The **Car** class outlined above is defined as a class template in the example on the next page with default attribute values.

An instance of the Car class is created in the example on page 88 with the custom values from the above outline.

Create an object

Object classes are normally declared before the main class in a Java program with just the "class" keyword.

Variables and methods are declared here with the "static" access modifier to be accessible in the main class.

These properties can be addressed with the object's class name followed by a dot and the given property name.

The example below creates an object class then displays its assigned values from the main method of the main class:

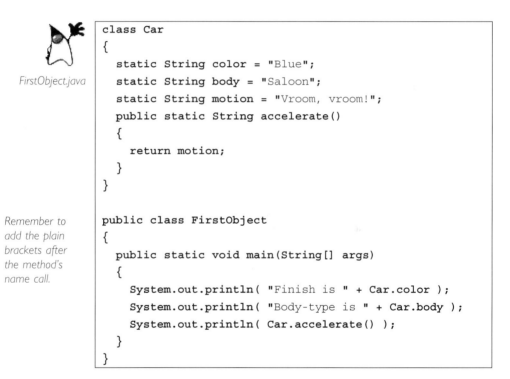

FirstObject.java

```java
class Car
{
  static String color = "Blue";
  static String body = "Saloon";
  static String motion = "Vroom, vroom!";
  public static String accelerate()
  {
    return motion;
  }
}

public class FirstObject
{
  public static void main(String[] args)
  {
    System.out.println( "Finish is " + Car.color );
    System.out.println( "Body-type is " + Car.body );
    System.out.println( Car.accelerate() );
  }
}
```

Remember to add the plain brackets after the method's name call.

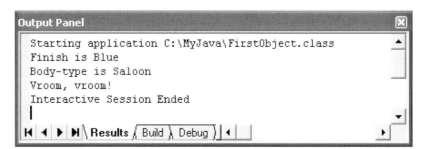

```
Output Panel                                    ⊠
  Starting application C:\MyJava\FirstObject.class  ▲
  Finish is Blue
  Body-type is Saloon
  Vroom, vroom!
  Interactive Session Ended
  |                                               ▼
  |◄ ◄ ► ►|\ Results ⟨ Build ⟩ Debug ⟩|◄  |     ►
```

Create an object instance

Each class has a built-in constructor method that can be used to create a new instance of that class.

The constructor method bears the same name as its class name and is invoked with the Java "new" keyword.

The program below builds on the previous example to create a new instance of the **Car** class then assigns it custom values:

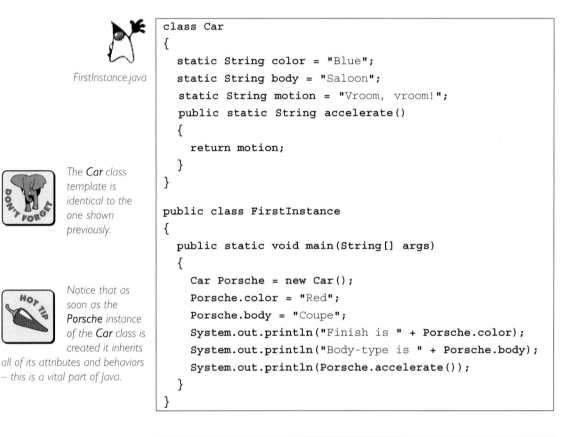

FirstInstance.java

```
class Car
{
  static String color = "Blue";
  static String body = "Saloon";
  static String motion = "Vroom, vroom!";
  public static String accelerate()
  {
    return motion;
  }
}

public class FirstInstance
{
  public static void main(String[] args)
  {
    Car Porsche = new Car();
    Porsche.color = "Red";
    Porsche.body = "Coupe";
    System.out.println("Finish is " + Porsche.color);
    System.out.println("Body-type is " + Porsche.body);
    System.out.println(Porsche.accelerate());
  }
}
```

The *Car* class template is identical to the one shown previously.

Notice that as soon as the *Porsche* instance of the *Car* class is created it inherits all of its attributes and behaviors – this is a vital part of Java.

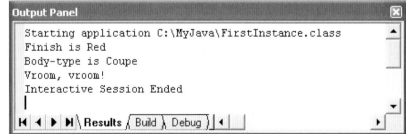

```
Output Panel                                              ☒
   Starting application C:\MyJava\FirstInstance.class    ▲
   Finish is Red
   Body-type is Coupe
   Vroom, vroom!
   Interactive Session Ended
   |                                                      ▼
 ◄◄ ◄ ► ►► \ Results / Build \ Debug } ◄              ►
```

Isolating objects

The object template class can be defined in a file other than that containing the program to make it more flexible.

When the program creates a new instance of that class it will automatically inherit the object's properties and values.

The concept of "inheritance" is used throughout the Java language to allow programs to use ready-made properties.

This program uses the isolated **Car** class that is embodied in its own file and could easily be used by other programs:

Car.class

```
class Car
{
  static String color = "Blue";
  static String body = "Saloon";
  static String motion = "Vroom, vroom!";
  public static String accelerate()
  {
    return motion;
  }
}
```

Instance.java

```
public class Instance
{
  public static void main(String[] args)
  {
    Car Diablo = new Car();
    Diablo.color = "Yellow";
    Diablo.motion = "Zoom, zoom!!!";
    System.out.print("The "+ Diablo.color + " Diablo");
    System.out.println(" went " + Diablo.accelerate());
  }
}
```

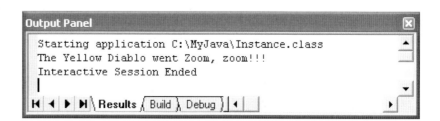

```
Output Panel                                              ☒
    Starting application C:\MyJava\Instance.class
    The Yellow Diablo went Zoom, zoom!!!
    Interactive Session Ended
    |
⏮ ◀ ▶ ⏭ \ Results ⟍ Build ⟍ Debug ⟍| ◀ |          ▶ |
```

Constant values

The "final" keyword is a modifier that can be used when declaring variables to prevent any subsequent change to the values that are initially assigned to them.

Because they are fixed these values are known as "constants" and it is convention to name constants with all uppercase characters to distinguish them from regular variables.

Programs that attempt to change a constant value will not compile and the compiler will generate an error message.

In the example below the **Car.COLOR** property is a constant value that cannot be assigned a new text string:

Constant.java

The "final" keyword modifier can also be used to declare constant methods.

```
class Car
{
  static final String COLOR = "Blue";
}

public class Constant
{
  public static void main(String[] args)
  {
    Car Ford = new Car();
    Ford.COLOR = "Red";
    System.out.println("Ford Color is " + Ford.COLOR);
  }
}
```

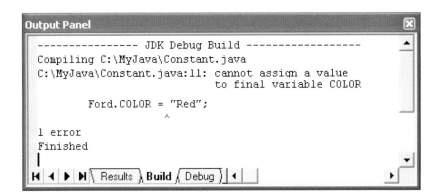

Encapsulation

The "private" keyword can be used when declaring object variables to protect their values from being directly changed by external program code.

Instead the object should include a method that enables the object variable values to be manipulated.

This technique of "encapsulation" is used in this example:

SafeInstance.java

```java
class Car
{
  private String color;
  private String body;
  public void setCar(String col, String bod)
  {
    color = col;  body = bod;
  }
  public void describeCar()
  {
    System.out.println("Finish is " + color);
    System.out.println("Body-type is " + body);
  }
}

public class SafeInstance
{
    public static void main(String[] args)
    {
    Car Bentley = new Car();
    Bentley.setCar("Gold","Saloon");
    Bentley.describeCar();
    }
}
```

The object in this example contains two attributes but no behaviors.

DON'T FORGET

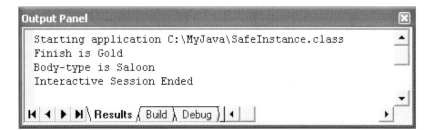

Output Panel

```
Starting application C:\MyJava\SafeInstance.class
Finish is Gold
Body-type is Saloon
Interactive Session Ended
```

⏮ ◀ ▶ ⏭ \ Results ⟨ Build ⟩ Debug ⟩ ◀

Initializer method

An object's constructor method can be called directly in the object class and is useful to initialize object variables.

This helps to keep the declarations and assignments separate and is good programming style.

In the following program four variables are declared then have values assigned by a constructor method:

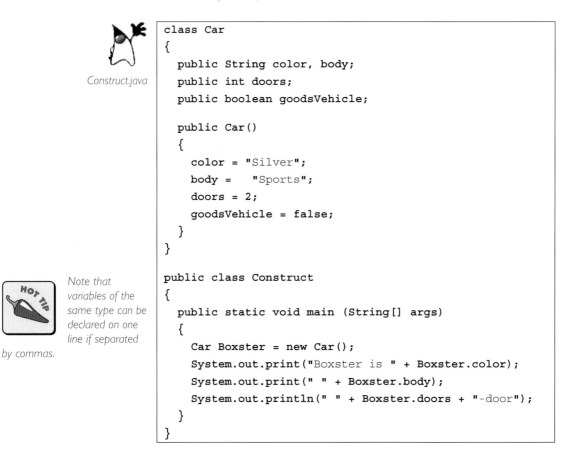

Construct.java

```java
class Car
{
  public String color, body;
  public int doors;
  public boolean goodsVehicle;

  public Car()
  {
    color = "Silver";
    body =   "Sports";
    doors = 2;
    goodsVehicle = false;
  }
}

public class Construct
{
  public static void main (String[] args)
  {
    Car Boxster = new Car();
    System.out.print("Boxster is " + Boxster.color);
    System.out.print(" " + Boxster.body);
    System.out.println(" " + Boxster.doors + "-door");
  }
}
```

Note that variables of the same type can be declared on one line if separated by commas.

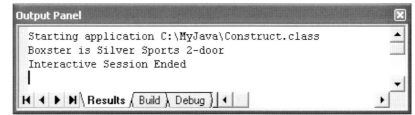

```
Output Panel                                              ☒
  Starting application C:\MyJava\Construct.class      ▲
  Boxster is Silver Sports 2-door                     ▮
  Interactive Session Ended
  |                                                   ▼
 ◄| ◄ ► |►\ Results / Build \ Debug / ◄|       ►
```

Handling errors

This chapter examines the sort of errors that can occur in Java programs and demonstrates how code can be introduced into the program to handle errors.

Covers

Chapter Nine

Compiler errors

It is inevitable that program authors will make human coding errors when creating Java programs.

Fortunately the Java compiler is designed to spot most of these errors and will not compile the program.

Instead, the Java compiler will helpfully report the line number of the error, the nature of the error, and also possibly a description of how the error may be corrected.

The compiler will only spot syntax errors – it does not pick up the second error in this example that attempts to output a non-existent array element.

The program below is erroneously attempting to assign an integer value to a **String** array.

This program does not compile and the compiler reports that it has found an **int** data type on line 5 where it expected to find a **String** data type.

The error location is pinpointed to make correction simple.

TypeError.java

```java
public class TypeError
{
    public static void main(String[] args)
    {
        String[] sport = {"Golf", "Polo", 100};
        System.out.println(sport[3]);
    }
}
```

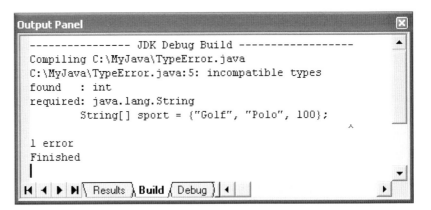

```
Output Panel                                          [x]

---------------- JDK Debug Build ------------------
Compiling C:\MyJava\TypeError.java
C:\MyJava\TypeError.java:5: incompatible types
found    : int
required: java.lang.String
        String[] sport = {"Golf", "Polo", 100};
                                          ^

1 error
Finished

|
|◄ ◄ ► ►|\ Results }\ Build / Debug }| ◄ |        ►
```

Runtime errors

The error reported by the compiler in the example on the facing page is easily corrected by replacing the **int** type assignment with a correct **String** type assignment.

Now the program will compile but when it runs the Java interpreter halts the execution and reports a further error.

Errors that occur at runtime are called "exceptions".

The exception is reported with the appropriate Java class that corresponds to the nature of the exception.

In the program below the exception is caused when the program attempts to output a non-existent array element.

There are many possible types of exception – this one is easily corrected by amending the code that addresses a non-existent array element.

This exception is therefore reported with the Java class called **ArrayIndexOutOfBoundsException**.

Like compiler error messages, the exception message will pinpoint the location of the exception within the program.

The exception message below indicates that the exception occurs on line 6 of the ArrayError program's main method:

ArrayError.java

```
public class ArrayError
{
  public static void main(String[] args)
  {
    String[] sport = {"Golf", "Polo", "Tennis"};
    System.out.println(sport[3]);
  }
}
```

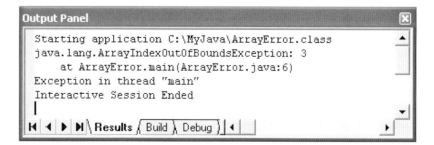

```
Output Panel                                              ☒
   Starting application C:\MyJava\ArrayError.class
   java.lang.ArrayIndexOutOfBoundsException: 3
       at ArrayError.main(ArrayError.java:6)
   Exception in thread "main"
   Interactive Session Ended
   |
  ⏮ ◀ ▶ ⏭ \ Results ⟨ Build ⟩ Debug ⟩| ◀        ▶
```

Catching an exception

Exceptions can often be caused by user input at runtime. For instance, the program below will echo an entered number but if the user mistakenly inputs a non-numeric argument an exception is reported at runtime.

If at all possible amend the program code to correct exceptions – only use a try-catch block to handle other exceptions.

```
public class Echo
{
  public static void main(String[] args)
  {
    float num = Float.parseFloat(args[0]);
    System.out.println("Input was "+num);
  }
}
```

This exception reports the **NumberFormatException** class.

The exception can be predicted and handled by enclosing the statements within a "try-catch" block with this syntax:

```
try  { /*statement(s) that may cause exception*/ }
catch ( Exception e ) { /* exception action(s)*/ }
```

Adding this block to the program above will then display a useful message when the user inputs a non-numeric entry:

Remember to add the letter "e" after the exception class name to denote the actual error.

```
public class Echo
{
  public static void main(String[] args)
  {
    try
    {
      float num = Float.parseFloat(args[0]);
      System.out.println("Input was "+num);
    }
    catch (NumberFormatException e)
    {
      System.out.println("Non-numeric entry");
    }
  }
}
```

With the program on the facing page, a further exception would occur if the user ran the program without any input.

In this case no arguments are entered so the **args** array does not have any elements and **args[0]** is non-existent.

This causes an **ArrayIndexOutOfBoundsException** error.

The try-catch block can be extended to also handle this kind of predictable exception by adding another catch statement:

Echo.java

```
public class Echo
{
  public static void main(String[] args)
  {
    try
    {
      float num = Float.parseFloat(args[0]);
      System.out.println("Input was "+num);
    }
    catch (NumberFormatException e)
    {
      System.out.println("Non-numeric entry");
    }
    catch (ArrayIndexOutOfBoundsException e)
    {
      System.out.println("Nothing entered");
    }
  }
}
```

Using try-catch to handle exceptions prevents Java interpreter exception messages.

Now this program will echo an entered numeric value or display an appropriate message if either exception occurs.

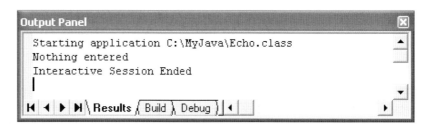

Output Panel

```
Starting application C:\MyJava\Echo.class
Nothing entered
Interactive Session Ended
```

Results / Build / Debug

After exceptions

The try-catch block can be extended by adding a "finally" block of statements that will always be executed.

A program will execute statements contained in the finally block irrespective of whether exceptions are found or not.

The example below adds a finally block onto the program on the previous page so it will always output a final message:

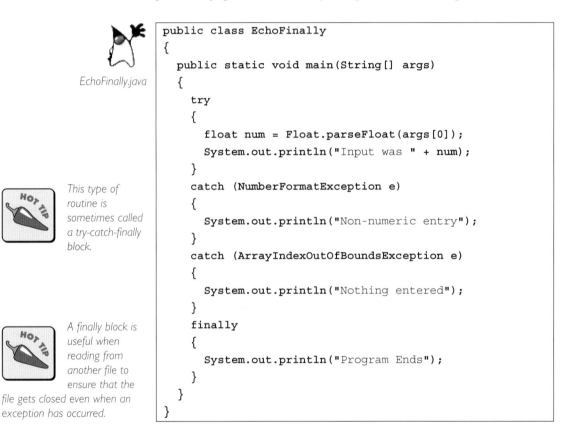

EchoFinally.java

This type of routine is sometimes called a try-catch-finally block.

A finally block is useful when reading from another file to ensure that the file gets closed even when an exception has occurred.

```java
public class EchoFinally
{
  public static void main(String[] args)
  {
    try
    {
      float num = Float.parseFloat(args[0]);
      System.out.println("Input was " + num);
    }
    catch (NumberFormatException e)
    {
      System.out.println("Non-numeric entry");
    }
    catch (ArrayIndexOutOfBoundsException e)
    {
      System.out.println("Nothing entered");
    }
    finally
    {
      System.out.println("Program Ends");
    }
  }
}
```

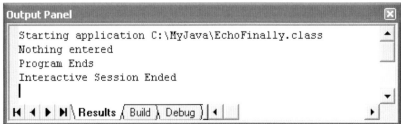

Output Panel

```
Starting application C:\MyJava\EchoFinally.class
Nothing entered
Program Ends
Interactive Session Ended
```

Results / Build \ Debug

Throwing exceptions

All exceptions in the previous examples are thrown by standard **java.lang** classes but any program can be made to throw its own exceptions.

First the Java "new" keyword is used to create an exception of the type **IllegalArgumentException()** and the exception message that it should display is stated as its only argument.

This exception can now be thrown with a "throw" keyword.

The program below creates a new exception that is thrown when the user enters a negative numerical value – for instance, -1.

The exception is caught by a catch block containing a statement that uses the exception's **getMessage()** method to display the exception message.

BePositive.java

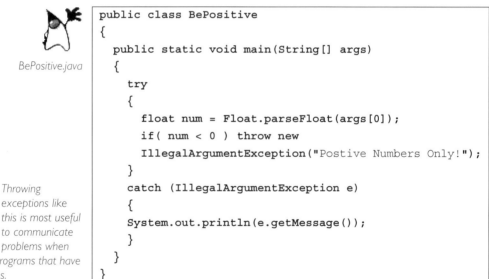

```java
public class BePositive
{
  public static void main(String[] args)
  {
    try
    {
      float num = Float.parseFloat(args[0]);
      if( num < 0 ) throw new
      IllegalArgumentException("Postive Numbers Only!");
    }
    catch (IllegalArgumentException e)
    {
    System.out.println(e.getMessage());
    }
  }
}
```

Throwing exceptions like this is most useful to communicate problems when working with programs that have multiple classes.

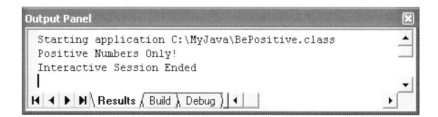

Output Panel

```
Starting application C:\MyJava\BePositive.class
Positive Numbers Only!
Interactive Session Ended
```

H ◀ ▶ ▶H \ Results \ Build \ Debug \ ◀

Passing exception responsibility

Responsibility for handling exceptions can be passed, from the method containing the exception, to the method that is calling it.

To pass this responsibility the "throws" keyword is added after the method declaration, followed by the name of the predicted exception to be handled.

In the program below, if the user enters "Five" an exception occurs in the **calc()** method but is handled by the **catch** statement in the main method:

ShowNum.java

```
public class ShowNum
{
 public static void main(String[] args)
 {
  try
  {
   System.out.println("Number is " + calc(args[0]) );
  }
  catch (NumberFormatException e)
  {
   System.out.println("Wrong format: " + e.getMessage());
  }
 }

 public static int calc(String num)
                        throws NumberFormatException
 {
  int number = Integer.parseInt(num);
  return number;
 }
}
```

This technique is especially useful with programs that call many methods that may create exceptions – they can all be handled in one try-catch block in the calling method.

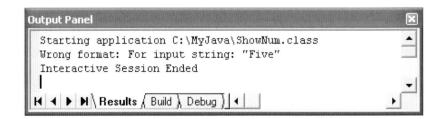

```
Output Panel                                          ☒
 Starting application C:\MyJava\ShowNum.class         ▲
 Wrong format: For input string: "Five"
 Interactive Session Ended
 |                                                    ▼
◄ ◄ ► ►◄ \ Results ⟨ Build ⟩ Debug ⟩ ◄               ►
```

Interface components

This chapter shows how to make Java programs that create windowed applications. Examples demonstrate how to add and layout each of the components that can be used to build a Graphical User Interface (GUI).

Covers

Chapter Ten

Creating a window

Java 2 makes it easy to create windows with the Swing class that is made available by declaring "import javax.swing.*;".

Remember the letter "x" in "javax.swing" by thinking of "JAVA eXtra".

A **JFrame** sub class of Java Swing creates window frames that can be resized, maximized, minimized and closed. A program can build the window in a class template that extends the **JFrame** class and specifies four features:

1.   The **super()** method takes a string argument that will appear on the window's title bar.

2.   The **setSize()** method takes two arguments that set the window's initial width and height.

The default close operation can be one of four JFrame constants; the one most used to close the application at the same time that the window closes is JFrame.EXIT_ON_CLOSE.

3.   The **setDefaultCloseOperation()** method takes a single argument to specify an action when the window closes.

4.   The **setVisible()** method takes a boolean argument of true to make the window actually appear.

The program's main method can then make an instance of the window's template class in order to produce a window.

HelloSwing.java

```java
import javax.swing.*;
class SwingWindow extends JFrame
{
  public SwingWindow()
  {
    super("Hello From Java Swing");
    setSize(300, 100);
    setDefaultCloseOperation(JFrame.EXIT_ON_CLOSE);
    setVisible(true);
  }
}

public class HelloSwing
{
  public static void main(String[] args)
  {
    SwingWindow Hello = new SwingWindow();
  }
}
```

Content containers

The previous program creates the window shown below that has all the usual window features – but lacks a content area.

Hello From Java Swing

To add a content area to this window requires a "container" to be included in the template class constructor block that will be able to display the window's content.

A **Container** class is included in Java's **Abstract Windowing Toolkit** class made available with "import java.awt.*;".

An instance of a **Container** class is created with the "new" Java keyword and the **getContentPane()** method.

The **Container** class has a **setBackground()** method that accepts a single argument to set its background color.

Adding the import declaration to the start of the previous program and the following two lines of code into its constructor method creates a content area container called "contentArea" that has a white background:

```
Container contentArea = getContentPane();
contentArea.setBackground(Color.white);
```

Hello From Java Swing

Adding push buttons

Positioning of interface components in a window is not specified absolutely by the program but should instead use a Java layout-manager.

This enables the Java windowed application to run without regard to the host operating system.

Layout-managers are covered in detail later in this chapter.

The layout-manager should be specified after the container is created in the window's constructor method.

Typically a program will specify the **FlowLayout** class that is part of the **Abstract Windowing Toolkit** as a layout-manager.

An instance of the **FlowLayout** class is created with the Java "new" keyword and the **FlowLayout()** method.

The container's **setLayout()** method then takes the name of the layout-manager as its argument to make the association.

Every graphical component that can be used in a Java windowed application is a class of either the **Swing** class or **Abstract Windowing Toolkit** class.

Components are added in the constructor block by creating new instances of their corresponding classes, which are then specified as the argument to the container's **add()** method.

Components are used in a program by setting their properties and calling their methods.

All of the components are finally applied to the container with the **setContentPane()** method that takes the name of the container as its sole argument.

Swing has a **JButton** class that is used in the program opposite to create interface push buttons in the Java Swing window that is illustrated below:

SwingButtons.java

```
import javax.swing.*;
import java.awt.*;

class SwingWindow extends JFrame
{
  public SwingWindow()
  {
    super("Push Buttons");
    setSize(300, 100);
    setDefaultCloseOperation(JFrame.EXIT_ON_CLOSE);
    setVisible(true);

    Container contentArea = getContentPane();
    contentArea.setBackground(Color.white);

    FlowLayout flowManager = new FlowLayout();
    contentArea.setLayout(flowManager);

    JButton playButton = new JButton("Play");
    contentArea.add(playButton);

    JButton pauseButton = new JButton("Pause");
    contentArea.add(pauseButton);

    JButton stopButton = new JButton("Stop");
    contentArea.add(stopButton);

    setContentPane(contentArea);
  }
}

public class SwingButtons
{
  public static void main(String[] args)
  {
    SwingWindow Buttons = new SwingWindow();
  }
}
```

Create the window

Create content container

Create layout-manager

Create interface components

HOT TIP *The following examples in this chapter replace the components in this program to illustrate other interface components.*

Adding labels and text fields

A label is a Java Swing component that may contain text or graphics to provide information about another component.

Typically the label will be text that instructs or advises the user how to treat the other component.

The label is created as an instance of the **JLabel** class using the Java "new" keyword and the **JLabel()** method. This method takes a string argument for the text to be displayed.

Often a label is used along with a text field component that allows the user to input text for use by the program.

A text field is created as an instance of the **JTextField** class using the Java "new" keyword and the **JTextField()** method.

This method must specify an argument to set the size of the text field as either an integer for the number of characters or a string that is to be initially displayed.

Optionally the method can take two arguments to specify both an integer size and an initial string.

The following lines replace the components in the earlier Push Buttons program to create a label and also a text field that has both a set size and an initial string:

TextNLabels.java
(part of)

```
JLabel textLabel = new JLabel("Fun Programming :");
contentArea.add(textLabel);

JTextField text = new JTextField("Java 2", 15);
contentArea.add(text);

setContentPane(contentArea);
```

The container in this example uses the default background color.

Text Fields and Labels

Fun Programming : Java 2

Checkboxes and radio buttons

Radio buttons and checkbox interface components can be added to allow the user to make selections.

Swing has a **JRadioButton** class and a **JCheckBox** class to create these components with the Java "new" keyword and the constructor method of the respective class.

Each of these methods takes a string argument to specify text to be displayed next to the component.

Both radio buttons and checkboxes can be combined into a **ButtonGroup** class so that only one button from the group can be selected at any given time.

The code below replaces the components in the earlier Push Buttons program to create a mutually exclusive group of three radio buttons and a single checkbox:

CheckRadios.java
(part of)

```
ButtonGroup wines = new ButtonGroup();
JRadioButton rad1 = new JRadioButton("Red");
JRadioButton rad2 = new JRadioButton("Rosé");
JRadioButton rad3 = new JRadioButton("White");
wines.add(rad1);
wines.add(rad2);
wines.add(rad3);
contentArea.add(rad1);
contentArea.add(rad2);
contentArea.add(rad3);

JCheckBox chk1 = new JCheckBox("Tick for details");
contentArea.add(chk1);

setContentPane(contentArea);
```

When grouping buttons they must first be added to the ButtonGroup then added to the container.

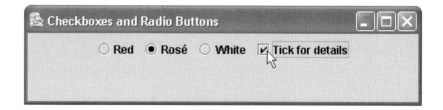

Combo boxes

A combo box is a useful component to provide a drop-down list from which the user may select a single item. The selected item is displayed in the component's main display.

Swing provides a **JComboBox** class to create this component using the "new" keyword and the **JComboBox()** method.

The **JComboBox** class has an **addItem()** method that, as its name suggests, is used to add items to the drop-down list.

When all items have been added, the container's **add()** method is used to include the entire combo box.

The code below replaces the components in the earlier Push Buttons program to create a combo box containing a drop-down list of some favorite Greek holiday destinations:

ComboBox.java
(part of)

```
JComboBox islands = new JComboBox();
islands.addItem("Corfu");
islands.addItem("Kefalonia");
islands.addItem("Crete");
islands.addItem("Rhodes");
islands.addItem("Paxos");
islands.addItem("Mykonos");

contentArea.add(islands);

setContentPane(contentArea);
```

Use combo boxes for longer selection lists to save space.

Slider components

A slider interface component allows the user to select a numeric value by dragging a selector across a scale of values.

Swing provides a **JSlider** class to create this component using the "new" keyword and the **JSlider()** method that takes two arguments to specify the start and finish of the range.

A final argument can be added to specify the position at which the selector should initially appear.

By default the slider will be created horizontally but can be made vertical by adding an initial argument to the **JSlider()** method specifying a constant called **JSlider.VERTICAL**.

The slider "tick" intervals are specified as arguments to methods of the **JSlider** class called **setMajorTickSpacing()** and **setMinorTickSpacing()**.

Remember to include the slider using the container's add() method.

These are applied to the display by specifying a true argument to the **setPaintTicks()** method of the **JSlider** class and labels can be displayed showing the value of major ticks with a true argument in the **setPaintLabels()** method.

This example replaces the components in the earlier Push Buttons program to create a horizontal slider:

Slider.java (part of)

```
JSlider scale = new JSlider(0, 100);
scale.setMajorTickSpacing(10);
scale.setMinorTickSpacing(5);
scale.setPaintTicks(true);
scale.setPaintLabels(true);
contentArea.add(scale);
setContentPane(contentArea);
```

Slider

0 10 20 30 40 50 60 70 80 90 100

Text areas

A text area is a useful component that enables the user to enter more than just a single line of text.

Swing provides a **JTextArea** class to create this component using the "new" keyword and the **JTextArea()** method.

This constructor method takes two arguments to specify the size of the text area to be created.

The first argument sets the height of the text area as a number of lines that it can display.

The second argument sets the width of the text area as the approximate number of characters each line can display.

Optionally a string argument can be added before the size arguments to specify an initial text string to be displayed.

The code below replaces the components in the earlier Push Buttons program to create a text area that is three lines high and 20 characters wide with an initial string to display:

Textarea.java
(part of)

```
JTextArea comments =
    new JTextArea("Please enter your comments", 3, 20);

contentArea.add(comments);

setContentPane(contentArea);
```

Text areas have no scrolling ability unless placed inside a scroll pane container.

TextArea

Please enter your comments

If the user enters text that exceeds the size of the component the area will expand to accommodate the text content. To make the area a fixed size with scrolling capabilities it should be placed in a scroll pane container as seen opposite.

A scroll pane component allows another component to scroll its content and so maintain a fixed interface size.

Swing provides a **JScrollPane** class to create this component using the "new" keyword and the **JScrollPane()** method.

This constructor method takes three arguments to specify the name of the component to be made scrollable, and when the horizontal and vertical scrollbars should appear.

The scrollbar requirement is specified with these constants:

JScrollPane.VERTICAL_SCROLLBAR_AS_NEEDED
JScrollPane.VERTICAL_SCROLLBAR_NEVER
JScrollPane.VERTICAL_SCROLLBAR_ALWAYS
JScrollPane.HORIZONTAL_SCROLLBAR_AS_NEEDED
JScrollPane.HORIZONTAL_SCROLLBAR_ALWAYS
JScrollPane.HORIZONTAL_SCROLLBAR_NEVER

The container's **add()** *method will include both the scroll pane and its specified component.*

The code below adds the text area opposite to a scroll pane that permanently displays both scrollbars. The container's **add()** method shown below replaces the previous one.

Scrollpane.java (part of)

```
JScrollPane scroller= new JScrollPane(comments,
   JScrollPane.VERTICAL_SCROLLBAR_ALWAYS,
   JScrollPane.HORIZONTAL_SCROLLBAR_ALWAYS);

contentArea.add(scroller);
```

Panel containers

A panel component is a simple container that is useful to divide an interface into different groups of components.

Swing provides a **JPanel** class to create this component using the "new" keyword and the **JPanel()** constructor method.

One major advantage of grouping components into panels is that each panel can specify its own layout-manager with its **setLayout()** method – to set the layout of its components.

Alternatively a layout-manager can be specified as an argument to the **JPanel()** constructor method.

The code below replaces the components in the earlier Push Buttons program to create two panel components.

These panels are set with different backgrounds for clarity and the buttons are added with the panel's **add()** method.

Panels.java
(part of)

Panels are useful to create an area in an interface to add a graphic or image – see

Chapter 14.

```java
JButton button1 = new JButton("Click Me");
JButton button2 = new JButton("Click Me");

JPanel panel1 = new JPanel();
panel1.setBackground(Color.white);
panel1.add(button1);

JPanel panel2 = new JPanel();
panel2.setBackground(Color.black);
panel2.add(button2);

contentArea.add(panel1);
contentArea.add(panel2);

setContentPane(contentArea);
```

Flow layout manager

The **FlowLayout** class layout-manager has been used to lay out components in all the previous examples in this chapter.

It lays out components in the same way that words flow across a page – from left to right, and onto the next line when the next component will not fit on the current line.

If the window area is increased more space becomes available on each line so the layout-manager will reposition the components to suit the new window size.

Notice the position of the buttons on the bottom line in each of the illustrations on this page. By default **FlowLayout** will center components in the available space.

Optionally the **FlowLayout()** constructor can accept an argument to align components to the left with the constant **FlowLayout.LEFT** or to the right with **FlowLayout.RIGHT**.

Also two further integer arguments can optionally be added to the **FlowLayout** constructor to specify the horizontal and vertical gap between components.

Border layout manager

The **BorderLayout** class layout-manager positions components into five designated areas.

These are specified as an argument to the container's **add()** method using one of the following **BorderLayout** constants:

BorderLayout.NORTH
BorderLayout.SOUTH
BorderLayout.EAST
BorderLayout.WEST
BorderLayout.CENTER

So **container.add(button2, BorderLayout.NORTH)** would position a component called "button2" on the topmost area.

Other components are positioned according to their specified compass value or in the remaining central area.

Because the **BorderLayout** class layout-manager utilizes all the available space the central area is usually the largest.

Component sequence does not affect this layout.

114 | Java in easy steps

Grid layout manager

A **GridLayout** class layout-manager will position all the components with an arrangement of rows and columns.

The numbers of rows and columns are specified as arguments to the **GridLayout()** constructor method.

For instance, **new GridLayout(2,3)** would create an arrangement that is two rows high and three columns wide.

The grid is created by dividing the total available space into cells of equal size irrespective of the size of each component.

Any components featuring text that exceeds the cell space will have their text truncated to fit the available space.

The **GridLayout** class layout-manager will fill each cell with components, in the same sequence in which they are added, working from left to right then wrapping to the next line.

In the example illustrated below the grid is created with two rows high and three columns wide. The first four cells are filled by push button components and the fifth cell houses a radio button component.

Place multiple components on a panel in order to control their position within a cell of the grid layout.

Grid Layout

| Button #1 | Button #2 | Button #3 |
| Button #4 | Radio Button #5 | |

Gridbag layout manager

A **GridBagLayout** class layout-manager can be used in place of the plain **GridLayout** class layout-manager to allocate components to specific cells in a grid.

This should be used together with a **GridBagConstraints** object that allows the component's position to be specified by its "gridx" and "gridy" attributes.

The arrangement of rows and columns is not specified as arguments to the constructor but is determined by the positions allocated by the various components.

Grid coordinates are numbered from zero up, so the example below creates a grid of 9 cells because the extreme component is button 3 at gridx=2, gridy=2.

GridBaglayout.java (part of)

```
GridBagLayout flowManager = new GridBagLayout();
GridBagConstraints pos = new GridBagConstraints();
contentArea.setLayout(flowManager);

JButton btn1 = new JButton("Button #1");
pos.gridx = 0; pos.gridy = 0;
contentArea.add(btn1, pos);

JRadioButton btn2=new JRadioButton("Radio Button #2");
pos.gridx = 1; pos.gridy = 1;
contentArea.add(btn2, pos);

JButton btn3 = new JButton("Button #3");
pos.gridx = 2; pos.gridy = 2;
contentArea.add(btn3, pos);

setContentPane(contentArea);
```

HOT TIP

The cell sizes will vary to suit the component – so the text with the radio button is not truncated.

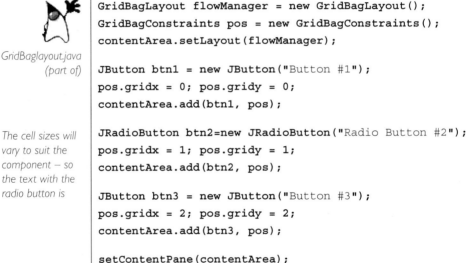

User interaction

This chapter demonstrates how to add features to a program that can handle user input from interface components or from the keyboard. Examples illustrate how user actions create events that can interact with a Java program.

Covers

Chapter Eleven

Listening for events

A user interacts with a program interface by performing actions with a mouse, keyboard or other input device.

These actions are called "events" and making a program respond to them is called "event handling".

In order for a program to recognize user events it needs to have one or more **Java EventListener** interfaces added from the "event" class of the **Abstract Windowing Toolkit**.

These are made generally available to the program with the **import java.awt.event.*;** header statement.

The required listener interfaces can then be added to the class declaration with the Java "implements" keyword.

For instance, the following declaration includes an **EventListener** that will recognize push button actions:

```
import javax.swing.*;
import java.awt.event.*;
class Click extends JFrame implements ActionListener{ }
```

There are different **EventListener** interfaces to recognize different events but the most popular, common ones that are used throughout this chapter are listed below:

Multiple listeners can be added after the "implements" keyword if they are separated by commas.

EventListener	Event
ActionListener	Button clicks
ItemListener	Check box item selections Radio button item selections Combo box item selections
KeyListener	Keyboard input
MouseListener MouseMotionListener	Mouse actions Mouse movements
ChangeListener (javax.swing.event)	Slider changes

Generating events

Components need to generate events that the **EventListener** interfaces can recognize if they are to be useful.

Having added the appropriate **EventListener** to the program, as described on the opposite page, an event generator method must be added to the component.

For instance, to respond to a button click, the **ActionListener** interface is added to the program and an **addActionListener()** method must be added to the button component itself.

The **addActionListener()** method takes a single argument using the Java "this" keyword to describe the action event.

So the code to create a button and enable it to generate a recognizable event would look like this:

```
JButton button = new JButton("Click Me");

button.addActionListener(this);
```

Now when a user clicks the button it will generate an event that automatically calls a method that should be added within the class where the component listener was added.

Each event listener has an associated method that is called when an event is generated by the user.

With the button example the **ActionListener** calls an associated method called **actionPerformed()**.

In the **actionPerformed()** declaration its argument should be specified as an object of a type called "ActionEvent".

This will receive the event description specified as the **addActionListener()** argument with the "this" keyword.

So an **ActionListener** event handler would look like this:

```
public void actionPerformed(ActionEvent event)
{
    /* add statements to be executed here */
}
```

Push button events

A single **actionPerformed()** event handler method can handle multiple action events in a program.

In order for the event handler to determine which component originated the event it must first examine the event description passed to it as an **ActionEvent** argument.

The **ActionEvent** object has a **getSource()** method that will return the given name of the originating component.

The buttons and text area are declared before the constructor method – to be globally available to the event handler method.

This is useful to identify the component generating the event so the program can execute appropriate statements.

The **ActionEvent** object also has a **getActionCommand()** method that will return a string from the component.

If the component is a button the string returned will be the text label on the button, or if the component is a text field the string returned will be the text content of that text field.

The program listed in full on the facing page adds action listeners to two button components.

When either button is pressed the **actionPerformed()** event handler first uses the **getActionCommand()** method to add the active button's text label to a String variable.

The event handler then uses the **getSource()** method to determine the originating button's identity and add an appropriate text message to the String variable.

Finally the complete text string is displayed using the **setText()** method of a text area component, as shown below:

```
Action Events                                    _ □ ✕

            Button #1      Button #2

         From: Button #2 - No.2
```

Actions.java

```
import javax.swing.*;
import java.awt.*;
import java.awt.event.*;

class Actions extends JFrame implements ActionListener
{
  JTextArea textarea = new JTextArea(2,25);
  JButton button1 = new JButton("Button #1");
  JButton button2 = new JButton("Button #2");

  public Actions()
  {
    super("Button Action");
    setSize(300, 100);
    setDefaultCloseOperation(JFrame.EXIT_ON_CLOSE);
    setVisible(true);

    Container content = getContentPane();
    FlowLayout layout = new FlowLayout();
    content.setLayout(layout);

    button1.addActionListener(this);
    button2.addActionListener(this);

    content.add(button1);
    content.add(button2);
    content.add(textarea);
    setContentPane(content);
  }

  public void actionPerformed(ActionEvent event)
  {
    String str="From: " + event.getActionCommand();
    if(event.getSource() == button1) str += "- No.1";
    if(event.getSource() == button2) str += "- No.2";
    textarea.setText(str);
  }

  public static void main(String[] args)
  { Actions eg = new Actions(); }
}
```

Create the components

Create the window

Create the container

Add the event listeners

Add the components

Add the event handler

Radio button events

The radio button components require the **ItemListener** interface to recognize user actions.

This interface is added from the "event" class of the **Abstract Windowing Toolkit** using the Java "implements" keyword.

Event listeners can be added to the components with the **addItemListener()** method so that they will generate events.

So the code to create a radio button and enable it to generate a recognizable event would look like this:

```
JRadioButton radOne = new JRadioButton("Number 1");

radOne.addItemListener(this);
```

Item events are handled by the **itemStateChanged()** method which takes an ItemEvent object as its single argument.

This receives the originating component object that is passed from the "this" keyword in the **addItemListener()** method.

An **ItemEvent** object has a **getItem()** method that can be used to identify the source of the event so that the program can execute appropriate statements.

The program listed in full on the facing page has a group of two radio buttons that generate an event and apply text to a label when they are selected by the user, as shown below:

Remember to add radio buttons to a ButtonGroup if they are to be made mutually exclusive.

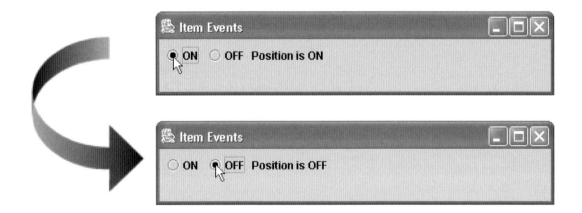

...cont'd

Items.java

Create the components

Create the window

Create the container

Add the event listeners

Add the components

Add the event handler

```java
import javax.swing.*;
import java.awt.*;
import java.awt.event.*;

class RadioItems extends JFrame implements ItemListener
{
  JRadioButton onBtn = new JRadioButton("ON");
  JRadioButton offBtn = new JRadioButton("OFF");
  JLabel position = new JLabel();

   public RadioItems()
   {
     super("Item Events"); setSize(300, 65);
     setDefaultCloseOperation(JFrame.EXIT_ON_CLOSE);
     setVisible(true);

     Container content = getContentPane();
     FlowLayout lay =new FlowLayout(FlowLayout.LEFT);
     content.setLayout(lay);

     onBtn.addItemListener(this);
     offBtn.addItemListener(this);

     ButtonGroup state = new ButtonGroup();
     state.add(onBtn); state.add(offBtn);
     content.add(onBtn);
     content.add(offBtn);
     content.add(position);
     setContentPane(content);
   }

  public void itemStateChanged(ItemEvent event)
  {
    if(event.getItem() == onBtn)
      position.setText("Position is ON");
    if(event.getItem() == offBtn)
      position.setText("Position is OFF");
  }

  public static void main(String[] args)
  { RadioItems eg = new RadioItems(); }
}
```

Checkbox events

Checkbox events require the **ItemListener** interface that is added just like the previous example for radio button events.

The event handler for checkboxes can usefully discern if the box is being checked or unchecked by each generated event.

An **ItemEvent** object has a **getStateChange()** method that will return an integer value. This value can be compared with constants called **ItemEvent.SELECTED** and **ItemEvent.DESELECTED** to determine the box's status.

The event handler below applies text to the box's text label appropriate to its current checked status:

CheckItems.java (part of)

```
public void itemStateChanged(ItemEvent event)
{
  int state = event.getStateChange();
  if(state == ItemEvent.SELECTED)
  {
  if(event.getItem() == redBox) redBox.setText("Red ON");
  if(event.getItem() == bluBox) bluBox.setText("Blue ON");
  }
  if(state == ItemEvent.DESELECTED)
  {
  if(event.getItem() == redBox)redBox.setText("Red OFF");
  if(event.getItem() == bluBox)bluBox.setText("Blue OFF");
  }
}
```

HOT TIP

The ItemEvent getStateChange() method returns 1 if selected and 2 if deselected.

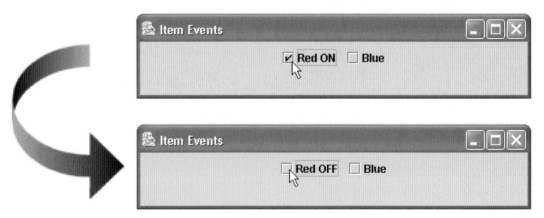

Combo box events

Combo box events require the **ItemListener** interface that is added just like the earlier example for radio button events.

The combo box's **addItemListener(this)** method statement adds the entire list of its items with just this one statement.

When the user selects an item from the drop-down list it is passed to the **itemStateChanged()** event handler method.

Components in this example have been left-aligned using the constant FlowLayout.LEFT parameter – see page 113.

The ItemEvent's **getItem()** method will retrieve the passed list **ItemEvent** object.

It is more useful to convert this to a string, using the **toString()** method, to reveal the item's listed text value.

The event handler shown below retrieves a selected list item then converts it to a string for display in a label:

ComboItems.java (part of)

```
public void itemStateChanged(ItemEvent event)
{
   String choice = event.getItem().toString();
   selection.setText("You Chose " + choice);
}
```

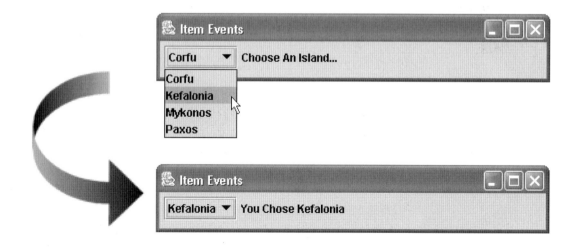

Slider events

The slider component requires the **ChangeListener** interface to recognize user actions.

This interface is made available from the "event" class of the Java Swing package using this header statement:

```
import javax.swing.event.*;
```

Comment out the first two lines of code in the program's event handler to have dynamic updating.

The Java "implements" keyword is used to add this **EventListener** to the program, and **addChangeListener(this)** is added to enable the slider component to generate events.

The slider event handler is the **StateChanged()** method that takes a **ChangeEvent** object as its argument.

While the slider is being adjusted it will repeatedly call that event handler to execute the code in its statement block.

This may be desirable to dynamically update a read-out but can be prevented with the **getValueIsAdjusting()** method.

The program opposite casts the slider source into a **JSlider** object so it can check the boolean return of this method.

When the user stops moving the selector the method returns false. Only then is the label text set, using the slider's **getValue()** method to return its actual position value.

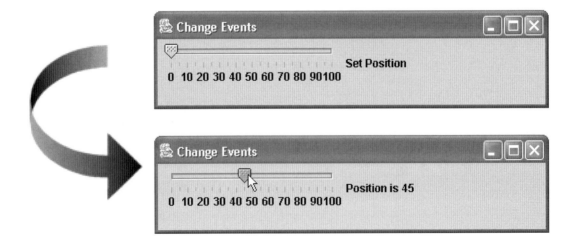

Changes.java

```java
import javax.swing.*;
import java.awt.*;
import javax.swing.event.*;

class Changes extends JFrame implements ChangeListener
{
```

Create the components

```java
  JSlider scale = new JSlider(0,100,0);
  JLabel position = new JLabel("Set Position");
```

```java
  public Changes()
  {
```

Create the window

```java
    super("Change Events"); setSize(300, 80);
    setDefaultCloseOperation(JFrame.EXIT_ON_CLOSE);
    setVisible(true);
```

Create the container

```java
    Container content = getContentPane();
    FlowLayout lay = new FlowLayout(FlowLayout.LEFT);
    content.setLayout(lay);
```

Configure slider component

```java
    scale.setMajorTickSpacing(10);
    scale.setMinorTickSpacing(5);
    scale.setPaintTicks(true);
    scale.setPaintLabels(true);
```

Add the event listener

```java
    scale.addChangeListener(this);
```

Add the components

```java
    content.add(scale);
    content.add(position);
    setContentPane(content);
  }
```

Add the event handler

```java
  public void stateChanged(ChangeEvent event)
  {
    JSlider src = (JSlider) event.getSource();
    if(!src.getValueIsAdjusting())
    position.setText("Position is "+ scale.getValue());
  }
```

```java
  public static void main(String[] args)
  { Changes eg = new Changes(); }
}
```

Keyboard events

Components that allow the user to input text can recognize individual keyboard strokes with the **KeyListener** interface.

This interface is added from the event class of the **Abstract Windowing Toolkit** using the Java "implements" keyword.

Event listeners can be added to the components with the **addKeyListener()** method so that they will generate events.

When a program implements the **KeyListener** interface it must specify these three event handler methods:

All three event handlers must be included – even if some are unused like those in the example opposite.

keyPressed(KeyEvent)	Called when a key is pressed
keyReleased(KeyEvent)	Called when a key is released
keyTyped(KeyEvent)	Called after a key is released

The **addKeyListener()** method takes the "this" keyword as its argument to pass the **KeyEvent** to the event handler.

Alphanumeric key characters can be assigned to a char type variable in the program using the **getKeyChar()** method.

The full program listed opposite gets the character on every keystroke and displays it in a label component.

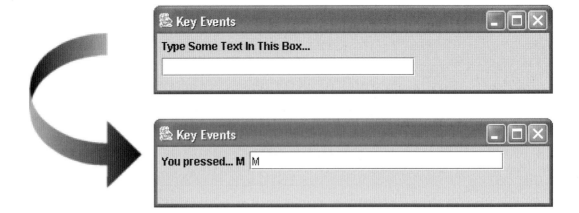

Keys.java

```java
import javax.swing.*;
import java.awt.*;
import java.awt.event.*;

class Keys extends JFrame implements KeyListener
{
```

Create the components

```java
  JLabel label =
        new JLabel("Type Some Text In This Box...");
  JTextField entry = new JTextField(25);
```

```java
  public Keys()
  {
```

Create the window

```java
    super("Key Events");
    setSize(300, 80);
    setDefaultCloseOperation(JFrame.EXIT_ON_CLOSE);
    setVisible(true);
```

Create the container

```java
    Container content = getContentPane();
    FlowLayout lay = new FlowLayout(FlowLayout.LEFT);
    content.setLayout(lay);
```

Add the event listener

```java
    entry.addKeyListener(this);
```

Add the components

```java
    content.add(label);
    content.add(entry);
    setContentPane(content);
  }
```

Add the event handlers

```java
  public void keyTyped(KeyEvent event)
  {
    char key = event.getKeyChar();
    label.setText("You pressed... " + key);
  }

  public void keyPressed(KeyEvent event)
  { /* this is an empty method */ }

  public void keyReleased(KeyEvent event)
  { /* this is an empty method */ }
```

```java
  public static void main(String[] args)
  { Keys eg = new Keys(); }
}
```

Mouse events

Program components can be made to recognize a user's mouse actions by including the **MouseListener** interface.

This interface is added from the event class of the **Abstract Windowing Toolkit** using the Java "implements" keyword.

Event listeners can be added to the components with the **addMouseListener()** method so they will generate events.

When a program implements the **MouseListener** interface it must specify these five event handler methods:

Rollover effects can be created by swapping images with mouseEntered() and mouseExited() methods.

mousePressed(MouseEvent)	Call when button is pressed
mouseReleased(MouseEvent)	Call when button is released
mouseClicked(MouseEvent)	Call after button is released
mouseEntered(MouseEvent)	Call when mouse moves on
mouseExited(MouseEvent)	Call when mouse moves off

The Java "this" keyword should be used as an argument in the **addMouseListener()** method to send the **MouseEvent** to the event handler.

If code is to be executed when a simple mouse click is detected then the **mouseClicked()** method should contain the statements that the event handler is to execute.

Where separate tasks are required when the button is pressed and released then the **mousePressed()** and **mouseReleased()** methods should be used instead.

Whenever the mouse pointer moves onto a component that has an added **MouseListener** the **mouseEntered()** event handler method is automatically called.

Similarly, whenever the mouse pointer is moved off a component that has a **MouseListener** the program will automatically call the **mouseExited()** event handler method.

Movements of the user's mouse can be tracked in a program by including the **MouseMotionListener** interface.

This interface is added from the event class of the **Abstract Windowing Toolkit** using the Java "implements" keyword.

Event listeners can be added to the components with the **addMouseMotionListener()** method to generate events.

The **addMouseMotionListener()** method takes the "this" argument to pass the **MouseEvent** to the event handler.

Tracking mouse coordinates can execute code only when the mouse is within specified coordinates.

When a program implements the **MouseListener** interface it must specify both a **mouseMoved(MouseEvent)** method and a **mouseDragged(MouseEvent)** method.

These are called when the user moves or drags the mouse.

The **mouseMoved()** event handler in the code below uses the MouseEvent's **getX()** and **getY()** methods to dynamically display the mouse coordinates as the user moves the mouse.

MouseMove.java

```java
public void mouseMoved(MouseEvent event)
{
  int xPos = event.getX();
  int yPos = event.getY();
  label.setText("Mouse at X =" + xPos + " Y =" + yPos);
}

public void mouseDragged(MouseEvent event)
{
  label.setText("Mouse Dragged");
}
```

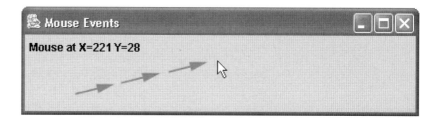

Disabling and enabling components

Components can be disabled with their **setEnabled()** method to prevent the user interacting with them.

This method takes a boolean value of either false, to disable the component, or true to enable the component.

Use this technique to ensure that a user has fully completed a form before proceeding.

Often this is useful to ensure that a user cannot skip through a procedure by disabling a button component that would allow the user to proceed. The program will only enable this button when the user has completed all prior requirements.

In the example below two buttons can toggle the enablement of a text field component. The user can only input or amend its text when that component is enabled.

*DisEnable.java
(part of)*

```
public void actionPerformed(ActionEvent event)
{
    boolean tog;
    tog = (event.getActionCommand() == "Disable") ?
        false : true;
    textBox.setEnabled(tog);
}
```

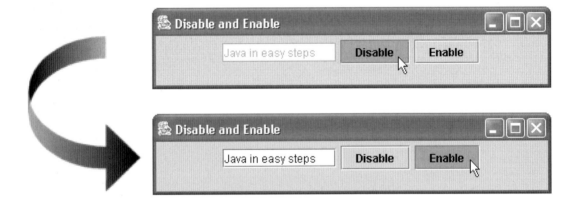

In the buttons' event handler this program uses the ActionEvent's **getActionCommand()** method to set a boolean variable depending on which button generated the event.

This is then used as the argument to the **setEnabled()** method.

Applets for the web

This chapter shows how to create Java programs that can be incorporated into a web page and run over the Internet. Examples illustrate how to allow features of the program to be customized from within the host HTML document.

Covers

Chapter Twelve

Introducing applets

An applet is a small program that is embedded inside another application and is not intended to run on its own.

The main appeal of Java applets is that they can be embedded into web pages to run across the Internet.

Java applets will run on any Java-enabled web browser – regardless of the operating system in use.

Modern web browsers can call upon the Java interpreter plugin to execute Java applets. This can be downloaded from **http://java.sun.com/products/plugin/** for those browsers which do not include it by default.

When a browser opens a web page that contains a Java applet the program files are downloaded into the browser's cache then the browser's Java interpreter attempts to run the applet.

It is important to keep the size of the applet files to a minimum in order to prevent lengthy downloads.

In Java 2, applets are an extension of the **JApplet** class that is part of the Java Swing Package, along with the Swing components.

The package is made available to the applet program with the usual header statement **import javax.swing.*;**.

Unlike windowed programs, the main class declaration in an applet must always include the "public" access modifier.

The class declaration should also use the "extends" keyword followed by "JApplet" to enable the program to inherit the methods and behaviors of the **JApplet** class.

Methods in the **JApplet** class are specially designed for use in applets and have security restrictions to prevent the applet being used maliciously.

The most noticeable difference between an applet and a regular program is that applets do not have a **main()** method.

Instead applets always have a method named **init()** that is called whenever the applet program starts.

The **init()** method can be used much like the constructor methods in previous examples to initialize variables and to add Swing components to the applet's interface.

The Hello World applet

A web page will display an applet program in a display area that is embedded between the other contents on that page.

By default this will appear as a light grey rectangle that is the blank canvas onto which text, Swing components, graphics and images can be painted by the applet program.

It is appropriate, therefore, that applets inherit a method named **paint()** from the **JApplet** class that can be used to paint text, shapes and graphics into the applet's display area.

Traditionally the Graphics object is just named "g", but the name "artist" helps explain its use.

The **paint()** method takes a single argument that is an instance of the Java **Graphics** class. This is the artist who knows how to render content onto the canvas.

The **Graphics** class is part of the **Abstract Windowing Toolkit** that must be made available to the applet program with the usual header statement **import java.awt.*;**.

The **drawString()** method of the **Graphics** class draws a string onto the canvas and takes as its arguments the string to be drawn, then the XY coordinates where to start drawing.

In the applet below, the **init()** method initializes a String variable that is drawn on the canvas by the **paint()** method.

HelloWorldApplet.java

There is no explicit call to the paint() method – it gets called spontaneously.

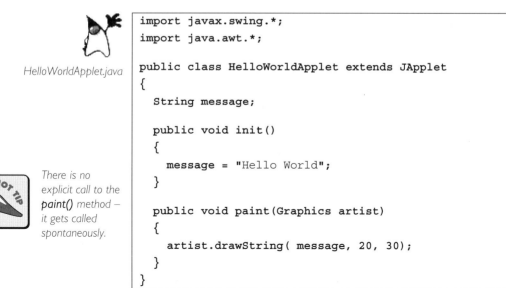

```java
import javax.swing.*;
import java.awt.*;

public class HelloWorldApplet extends JApplet
{
  String message;

  public void init()
  {
    message = "Hello World";
  }

  public void paint(Graphics artist)
  {
    artist.drawString( message, 20, 30);
  }
}
```

Embedding in a web page

To embed a Java applet in a web page the HTML code must specify the name of the applet file and the size of the applet's display area that is to be allocated on the page.

This information is specified in the body of the web page with attributes of the HTML <applet> tag.

A "code" attribute is assigned the name of the compiled applet file including its **.class** file extension.

All attribute values should be enclosed in double quotes.

A "width" attribute is assigned a numeric value that determines the width in pixels of the applet's display area.

A "height" attribute is assigned a numeric value that determines the height in pixels of the applet's display area.

The <applet> tag has an associated </applet> closing tag.

Optionally this pair of tags can surround a text message that will only be displayed if the applet cannot be executed.

The example HTML code shown below embeds the "HelloWorldApplet" from the previous page into a web page.

A default message is included and attributes allocate a canvas size of 300 x 60 pixels in which the applet will run.

HelloWorldApplet.html

```html
<html>

<head>
<title>Hello World Applet</title>
</head>

<body>

<applet code = "HelloWorldApplet.class"
        width = "300" height = "60">

You require a Java-enabled browser to view this applet.

</applet>

</body>

</html>
```

Testing with AppletViewer

The Java SDK includes an application called AppletViewer that can be used to test compiled applet programs with the Java interpreter which is installed along with the Java SDK.

Both the HTML file and the compiled applet file should be saved together in a directory that is on the Java path.

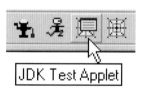

AppletViewer will display the applet but not other content in a web page.

For instance, the **HelloWorldApplet.class** file and the **HelloWorldApplet.html** file from the previous two pages were saved in a directory at **C:\MyJava**.

The applet can now be tested from a command prompt in that directory by typing **appletviewer** followed by a space and the name of the HTML file:

```
C:\MyJava>appletviewer HelloWorldApplet.html
```

In JPadPro the applet can be tested by selecting the menu items JDK > Test Applet, then typing the path and file name of the HTML file in the "Confirm File" dialog box that appears.

Alternatively click the toolbar button that is situated to the right of the JDK Interpreter button then browse to the file.

Whatever method is used, the AppletViewer application will open a window that displays the HelloWorldApplet program.

```
Applet Viewer: HelloWorldApplet.class
Applet

   Hello World

Applet started.
```

Setting applet parameters

Parameters provide a means to introduce custom values into a Java applet from within the HTML code of a web page.

The parameter information is specified in <param> tags that must be contained between the main <applet> tags and always have two attributes called "name" and "value".

Each parameter should assign a unique name to its "name" attribute while the actual data to be used in the applet is assigned to its "value" attribute.

The data is retrieved from the applet with a **getParameter()** method that takes the parameter name as its single argument.

ParamApplet.java

```java
import javax.swing.*;
import java.awt.*;

public class ParamApplet extends JApplet
{
  String car, acc, max, pic;

  public void init()
  {
    car = getParameter("superCar");
    acc = getParameter("holdOn");
    max = getParameter("flatOut");
    pic = getParameter("picture");
  }

  public void paint(Graphics artist)
  {
    if( car != null && acc != null && max != null)
    {
    artist.drawString( car, 5,145);
    artist.drawString("0-60 mph - "+acc, 135,160);
    artist.drawString("Top Speed - "+max+" mph",5,160);
    }

    Image photo = getImage( getCodeBase(), pic);
    if(photo != null) artist.drawImage(photo,5,5,this);
  }
}
```

Declare several variables, of the same type, on a single line by separating them with commas.

Applet parameters provide string values which are typically retrieved in the **init()** method and assigned to variables.

To be sure that the parameter value has been supplied the applet should always check that the assigned value is not null before using it in the program.

For more on displaying images with Java refer to page 164.

In the example shown here the HTML code specifies four parameter values.

The applet's **init()** method assigns the parameter values to string variables that are used to display text and an image.

Each of these attribute values could be quickly changed to display a different car's image and performance data.

ParamApplet.html (part of)

```
<applet code = "ParamApplet.class"
        width = "300" height = "60">
<param name="superCar" value="Porsche Carrera Turbo">
<param name="holdOn" value="3.7 seconds">
<param name="flatOut" value="174">
<param name="picture" value="porsche.gif">

You require a Java-enabled browser to view this applet.
</applet>
```

Swing components in applets

Swing components can be used in Java applets in the same way that they are used in windowed applications.

The applet creates its own window to which the **init()** method is used to add the components.

This example toggles the text on a button when it is clicked:

SwingApplet.java

```java
import java.awt.*; import java.awt.event.*;
import javax.swing.*;

public class SwingApplet extends JApplet
                                implements ActionListener
{
  JButton button;

  public void init()
  {
    Container contentArea = getContentPane();
    FlowLayout layout=new FlowLayout(FlowLayout.LEFT);
    contentArea.setLayout(layout);

    button = new JButton("Click Me");
    button.addActionListener(this);
    contentArea.add(button);
    setContentPane(contentArea);
  }

  public void actionPerformed(ActionEvent e)
  {
    if(e.getActionCommand() == "Click Me")
    button.setText("Thank You");
    else button.setText("Click Me");
  }
}
```

Create a container

Create components

Add event handler

Applet Viewer:	Applet Viewer: SwingApplet.class
Applet	Applet
Click Me	**Thank You**
Applet started.	Applet started.

Applet methods

Java applets inherit several methods from the **JApplet** class that are designed to be especially useful on the Internet.

The most frequently used applet methods are **init()** and **paint()** that are used to create the applet display.

Other applet methods offer the means to utilize remote resources from the web inside the applet program.

The table below lists applet methods with a description of how they may be used:

The code example on page 138 uses the getCodeBase() method with the getImage() method to display an image.

Method	Use
init()	Set up colors, fonts, variables & components when first loaded
paint()	Display text, shapes & graphics
repaint()	Call paint() for an update
start()	Start a process eg: animation
stop()	Halt a process
destroy()	Restore a state before exiting
showStatus(String msg)	Show this text in the status bar
getParameter(String name)	Get this named parameter value
getCodeBase()	Get location of the web page
getImage(URL url)	Get an image file from this URL
getAudioClip(URL url)	Get a sound file from this URL
play(URL url)	Play a sound file at this location

Optionally the **getImage()**, **getAudioClip()** and **play()** methods can accept a second String argument to name the resource that is sought.

Preparing applets for the web

The AppletViewer application that is used to test applets employs the Java interpreter that is part of the Java 2 SDK.

Although this supports Java 2, web browsers may use their own intrinsic Java interpreter which may not support Java 2.

This could mean that applets using the Java 2 language would not run correctly on those browsers.

However, Sun Microsystems have a plugin application that can be used to run Java 2 applets in any browser.

The plugin is part of the Java Runtime Environment that gets installed with the Java SDK and is available separately for download at **http://java.sun.com/products/plugin**.

http://java.sun.com

It is important to note that the plugin is a Java interpreter that is installed in addition to the browser's own intrinsic interpreter.

So even if the user has the plugin installed on their system the web browser will still attempt to run an applet with its intrinsic default interpreter.

The solution is to amend the HTML code to force the web browser to use the plugin instead of its default interpreter.

This can be done manually but is quite complex and requires separate pieces of HTML code for Netscape and Internet Explorer.

For simplicity Sun Microsystems have an application called **HTML Converter** that will make the necessary changes to the HTML code automatically.

This is a Java application that is available for all platforms that support Java.

It will change the code on a web page containing an applet to ensure that the web browser will only run the applet with the Java plugin that supports Java 2.

The **HTML Converter** application is included with the Java 2 SDK and is also available for free download from Sun Microsystems at **http://java.sun.com/products/plugin**.

The **HTML Converter** application is located in the **C:\Java\bin** directory, or can be downloaded from Sun Microsystems and placed there.

The application interface is started at a command prompt from within its host directory simply by typing the application name:

Browse to the HTML file in which the applet code is embedded then click the "Convert" button to make the changes. **HTML Converter** will make a back-up copy of the file then search for the <applet> tags in the HTML code and replace them automatically with the new HTML code.

Viewing applets in a browser

The entire contents of the <applet> element in the **HelloWorldApplet.html** file (listed on page 136) is converted by **HTML Converter** to the <object> element listed below:

HelloWorldApplet.html
(part of – converted)

```
<OBJECT WIDTH = "300" HEIGHT = "60"
classid = "clsid:8AD9C840-044E-11D1-B3E9-00805F499D93"
codebase = "http://java.sun.com/products/plugin/autodl/
          jinstall-1_4-windows-i586.cab#Version=1,4,0,0">

<PARAM NAME = CODE VALUE = "HelloWorldApplet.class" >
<PARAM NAME = "type"
        VALUE = "application/x-java-applet;version=1.4">
<PARAM NAME = "scriptable" VALUE = "false">

<COMMENT>
<EMBED type = "application/x-java-applet;version=1.4"
CODE = "HelloWorldApplet.class"
WIDTH = "300" HEIGHT = "60" scriptable = false
pluginspage =
      "http://java.sun.com/products/plugin/index.html">
  <NOEMBED>
  You require a Java-enabled browser to view this applet.
  </NOEMBED>
</EMBED>
</COMMENT>
</OBJECT>
```

In the event that the plugin is not installed the web page can display the default text in the <noembed> tag in place of the applet.

After the HTML file, applet **.class** file and any other associated files have been uploaded to a web server, the applet can be viewed on that HTML page by any web browser.

More applet examples are given in later chapters of this book.

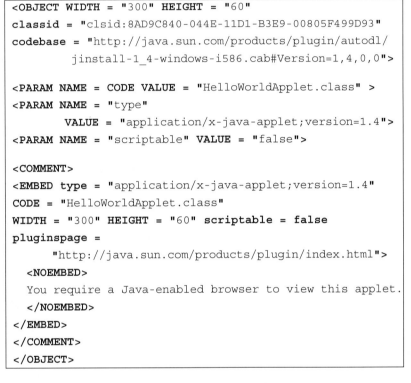

Fonts, colors and shapes

This chapter explores how to specify fonts and colors in Java applications and applets. Examples also demonstrate how to create lines, circles, rectangles and other exciting color graphics.

Covers

Chapter Thirteen

Creating font objects

In order to specify a display font, a **Font** object must first be created to contain information about the required font.

The **Font** class is part of the **Abstract Windowing Toolkit** and its constructor method has this syntax:

```
Font( font-name, font-style, font-size );
```

The font name should be one of the three platform-independent names "Serif", "SansSerif" or "Monospaced".

Multiple font style constants can be specified with the "+" operator – i.e. for bold italic text use Font.BOLD+Font.ITALIC.

The font style is specified with the three constants **Font.PLAIN**, **Font.BOLD** and **Font.ITALIC**.

The font size should be an integer of the required point size.

Typically fonts might be set up in the program's constructor method, or in the **init()** method with applets.

Once a **Font** object has been created it can be applied to each component as the argument to their **setFont()** method.

For instance, the code below creates a **Font** object that is then applied to a label component:

```
JLabel label = new JLabel("Serif Font.PLAIN, 32");

Font customFont = new Font("Serif", Font.PLAIN, 32);
label1.setFont( customFont );
```

This illustration shows three labels that have a variety of fonts applied.

Creating color objects

The easiest way to specify a display color is with one of the constant values from the Java **Color** class, which can be any of the following colors: black, blue, cyan, darkGray, gray, green, lightGray, magenta, orange, pink, red, white, yellow.

To specify a custom color, a **Color** object must first be created to contain information about the required color.

The **Color** class is part of the **Abstract Windowing Toolkit** and its constructor method has this syntax:

```
Color( red-value, green-value, blue-value );
```

If a specified RGB color is not exactly available the browser will use an approximate near color automatically.

These three arguments state how much red, green and blue is present in the color – each on a scale from 0 to 255.

When all three values are zero the color is black.

Adding to each value increases each color, so RGB values of 128 red, 0 green, 128 blue produce the color purple.

Each color is added like light, changing shades until white is reached with all three values at 255.

The example below applies a custom color to the background of a button using its setBackground() method. A **Color** constant is then applied to the foreground of the same button using its **setForeground()** method.

```
JButton button = new JButton("This Is A Purple Button");
Color customPurple = new Color(128,0,128);
button.setBackground(customPurple);
button.setForeground(Color.white);
```

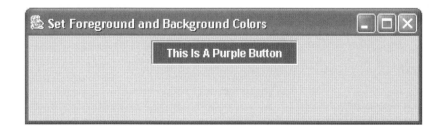

Painting applet fonts and colors

Java applets automatically call a method named **paint()** whenever the applet program is run.

This method takes a **Graphics** context as its sole argument.

A **Graphics** context has methods that can be used to paint fonts, colors and text onto the applet display area.

The **Graphics** context's **setColor()** method takes a **Color** object as its argument to set the color with which to paint.

The applet area's background can be painted in the currently set color using the **Graphics** context's **fillRect()** method.

This method takes four arguments and has this syntax:

```
fillRect( X, Y, width, height );
```

The first two arguments specify the XY coordinates of the top left corner of a rectangle that is to be filled with color, and the last two arguments determine its size.

In order to fill the entire area the XY coordinates should each be set at zero to denote a point at the extreme top left corner of the applet's display area.

The repaint() method can also call paint() to update the applet.

The other two arguments can be set with integer values of the applet size but this does not allow for possible resizing.

To ensure that the entire area is filled the last two arguments can be specified with **getSize().width** and **getSize().height**.

So a complete statement would look like this:

```
fillRect( 0, 0, getSize().width, getSize().height );
```

A **Graphics** context also has a **setFont()** method that takes a **Font** object argument to specify a font to paint with.

The text specified as the argument to the **Graphics** context's **drawString()** method will be painted onto the applet display area in the currently set font and color.

The applet shown below fills the entire background with yellow color then sets a font before painting one text string in red color, then another in blue color.

If the applet window is resized the **paint()** method is called again to repaint the background and text strings.

PaintApplet.java

```java
import javax.swing.*; import java.awt.*;

public class PaintApplet extends JApplet
{
    String msg;
    public void init()
    {
        msg = "This Is A Painted Applet";
    }

    public void paint(Graphics painter)
    {
        painter.setColor(Color.yellow);
        painter.fillRect(0,0,
                    getSize().width,getSize().height);

        Font myFont=new Font( "Serif",Font.ITALIC,28 );
        painter.setFont(myFont);

        painter.setColor(Color.red);
        painter.drawString(msg,10,25);

        painter.setColor(Color.blue);
        painter.drawString("With 3 Different
                                    Colors",10,52);
    }
}
```

Paint a yellow background

Set a custom font

Paint a red string

Paint a blue string

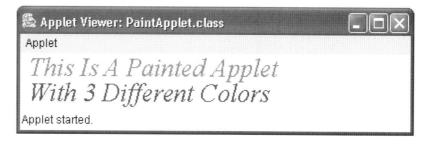

Painting application fonts and colors

Java applications automatically call a method named **paintComponent()** whenever the application is run.

This method takes a **Graphics** context as its sole argument that can be used to paint fonts, colors and text onto a panel.

The **paintComponent()** method should be contained inside an inner class that extends the **JPanel** class.

An instance of the inner class can then be added to the program's constructor method.

The **Graphics** context's **setColor()** method takes a **Color** object as its argument to set the color with which to paint.

The panel's background can be painted in the currently set color using the **Graphic** context's **fillRect()** method.

This method takes four arguments and has this syntax:

```
fillRect( X, Y, width, height );
```

To fill the entire panel the XY coordinates should each be set at zero, denoting the panel's top left corner, and the dimensions set with **getSize().width** and **getSize().height**.

The repaint() method can also call the paintComponent() method to update the application.

A custom font can be specified as the argument to the **Graphics** context's **setFont()** method and a text string can be painted onto the panel with its **drawString()** method.

The program listed in full on the opposite page paints a white background and a purple text string onto a panel component.

If the window is resized the panel is repainted automatically.

Painted Panel

This Is A Painted Panel

PaintPanel.java

Create the window

Create the container

Add the components

Paint a white background

Set a custom font

Paint a purple string

```java
import java.awt.*;
import javax.swing.*;

public class PaintPanel extends JFrame
{
    public PaintPanel()
    {
        super("Painted Panel");
        setSize(300, 100);
        setDefaultCloseOperation(JFrame.EXIT_ON_CLOSE);
        setVisible(true);

        Container contentArea = getContentPane();

        CustomPanel panel = new CustomPanel();
        contentArea.add(panel);
        setContentPane(contentArea);
    }

    class CustomPanel extends JPanel
    {
        public void paintComponent(Graphics painter)
        {
            painter.setColor(Color.white);
            painter.fillRect(0,0,getSize().width,
                                    getSize().height);

            Font currentFont=new Font("Serif",Font.BOLD, 24);
            painter.setFont(currentFont);

            Color customPurple = new Color(128,0,128);
            painter.setColor(customPurple);
            painter.drawString("A Painted Panel",20,40);
        }
    }

    public static void main(String[] arguments)
    { PaintPanel eg = new PaintPanel(); }
}
```

The statement block in the **paintComponent()** method of this program is used by the examples on the following pages in this chapter that illustrate how to draw graphics.

Drawing lines

The ability to draw lines is made available to programs with the header **import java.awt.geom.*;**

Graphics can be painted using the **paintComponent()** method, like the font and colors in the previous example.

However, the methods needed to draw graphics are not contained in the regular **Graphics** context, but rather in a class named **Graphics2D** contained in **java.awt.geom**.

The regular **Graphics** context can be simply cast into a **Graphics2D** context to make the required methods available.

A line can now be created as a **Line2D.Float** object.

The line's constructor takes two sets of coordinates for the desired start and end points of the line.

The coordinates take the form of (x1, y1, x2, y2) and are specified as floating-point values for greater accuracy.

Finally the **draw()** method of the **Graphics2D** context takes the line as its argument to draw it on the component.

The code below replaces the **paintComponent()** method in the previous example to illustrate a single line:

The top panel in the previous example has been removed – to show all the following graphics examples in a single panel.

```java
public void paintComponent(Graphics painter)
{
    Graphics2D painter2D = (Graphics2D) painter;
    Line2D.Float line1=new Line2D.Float(30F,30F,270F,30F);
    painter2D.draw(line1);
    painter2D.drawString("Here Is A 1-Pixel Line", 30, 25);
}
```

Draw Lines Demo

Here Is A 1-Pixel Line

The default line thickness when drawing graphics is 1 pixel but this can be changed to become thicker.

This technique requires the **BasicStroke** class that is contained in the **Abstract Windowing Toolkit** package.

Remember to import the java.awt.geom.* class to make all Graphics2D methods available.

The constructor method of this class takes a single integer argument that specifies the required line thickness in pixels.

A **Graphics2D** method named **setStroke()** then takes the **BasicStroke** object as its argument to change the thickness.

Any lines drawn subsequently will have the new thickness until another thickness is set.

The example below builds on the example on the facing page to draw a second line that is 10 pixels thick:

DrawLinesDemo.java

```
public void paintComponent(Graphics painter)
{
   Graphics2D painter2D = (Graphics2D) painter;
   Line2D.Float line1=new Line2D.Float(30F,30F,270F,30F);
   painter2D.draw(line1);

   painter2D.drawString("Here Is A 1-Pixel Line",30,25);

   BasicStroke pen = new BasicStroke(10);
   painter2D.setStroke( pen );
   Line2D.Float line2=new Line2D.Float(30F,60F,270F,60F);
   painter2D.draw(line2);

   painter2D.drawString("Here Is A 10-Pixel Line",30,50);
}
```

Notice that the drawString() method is not affected by the line thickness.

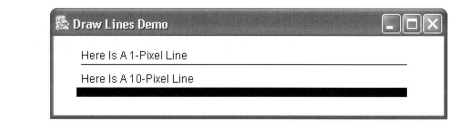

Drawing rectangles

The ability to draw geometric shapes is made available to programs with the header **import java.awt.geom.*;**.

A program can use the **Rectangle2D.Float()** method from this class to create rectangular shapes.

This method takes four arguments with this syntax:

```
Rectangle2D.Float( X, Y, width, height );
```

The first two arguments specify the XY coordinates where the top left corner of the rectangle should start.

Then the specified width and height arguments are measured from that point to determine the overall size.

All arguments must be stated as floating-point values which allows the position of the rectangle to be fixed accurately.

The rectangle will be drawn with the default line thickness of 1 pixel, unless the **BasicStroke()** size has been set.

The example below replaces the **paintComponent()** method in the example on page 151 to illustrate a simple rectangle:

DrawRectangle.java
(part of)

```java
public void paintComponent(Graphics painter)
{
  Graphics2D painter2D = (Graphics2D) painter;
  Rectangle2D.Float box =
          new Rectangle2D.Float(30F, 30F, 240F, 30F);
  painter2D.draw(box);
  painter2D.drawString("A Simple Rectangle", 30, 25);
}
```

*The first line of this method casts the **Graphics** context to a **Graphics2D** context.*

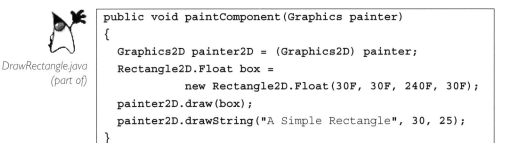

Rounding and filling

Rectangles with rounded corners can be created with the **RoundRectangle2D.Float()** constructor method that is contained in the **java.awt.geom** class.

This method is similar to the plain **Rectangle2D.Float()** method but adds two further arguments.

These specify the distance in pixels away from the corners that the rounding should begin in the X and Y directions.

So the method's full syntax looks like this:

```
RoundRectangle2D.Float( X, Y, W, H, +X, +Y );
```

A fill() method can be used in place of draw() with any shape.

Using the default stroke thickness the **Graphics2D draw()** method draws the rounded rectangle with a 1-pixel outline.

Alternatively the **Graphics2D fill()** method can be used to draw the rounded rectangle filled with the current color.

The example below builds on that shown on the facing page to create a rounded filled rectangle:

DrawRoundedRectangle.java (part of)

```java
public void paintComponent(Graphics painter)
{
  Graphics2D painter2D = (Graphics2D) painter;
  painter2D.drawString("Rounded Filled Rectangle",30,25);
  RoundRectangle2D.Float box =
    new RoundRectangle2D.Float(30F,30F,230F,30F,15F,15F);
  painter2D.setColor(Color.lightGray);
  painter2D.fill(box);
}
```

Draw Rounded Rectangle Demo

Rounded Filled Rectangle

Ellipses and circles

Both circles and ellipses can be created with the **Ellipse2D.Float()** constructor method that is contained in the **java.awt.geom** class.

To make this method available to a program requires that the header statement **import java.awt.geom.*;** is added.

The method takes four arguments with the following syntax:

A circle is just an ellipse that has equal width and height.

```
Ellipse2D.Float( X, Y, width, height );
```

Note that the XY coordinates do not place the centre of the ellipse but the position of the top left corner of an invisible rectangle into which an ellipse will exactly fit.

The width and height determine the size of the invisible rectangle, and therefore the size of the ellipse it contains.

The code below replaces the **paintComponent()** method on page 151 to demonstrate a circle and an ellipse:

*DrawEllipse.java
(part of)*

This example code omits the drawString() methods – to save on space.

```java
public void paintComponent(Graphics painter)
{
  Graphics2D painter2D = (Graphics2D) painter;
  Ellipse2D.Float ring1 =
          new Ellipse2D.Float(45F, 20F, 45F, 45F );
  painter2D.draw(ring1);
  Ellipse2D.Float ring2 =
          new Ellipse2D.Float(150F, 20F, 100F, 45F );
  painter2D.setColor(Color.lightGray);
  painter2D.fill(ring2);
}
```

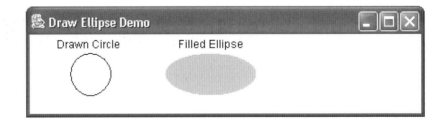

Drawing arcs

Arc shapes can be drawn in Java with the **Arc2D.Float()** method from the **java.awt.geom** class.

This works like the **Ellipse2D.Float()** method to create an invisible rectangle to contain a circle.

There are three additional arguments to the method that specify where on the circle the arc should begin, the size of the arc in degrees and the type of arc to draw.

```
Arc2D.Float( X, Y, width, height, start, size, type );
```

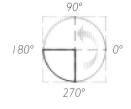

For reference, the circle is divided into 360 degrees with the zero degree positioned confusingly at 3 o'clock on the circle.

Degrees are counted around the circle anticlockwise.

The start point argument to the **Arc2D.Float()** method should specify the degree point from which to start the arc.

An arc type must be specified as either PIE, CHORD or OPEN using **Arc2D.Float** class constants.

The code sample below shows statements that produce the PIE arc shown in the following illustration.

```
Arc2D.Float arc1 = new Arc2D.Float
            (20F,10F,45F,45F,180F,90F,Arc2D.Float.PIE);
painter2D.draw(arc1);
```

DrawArc.java
(part of)

This code is repeated with different coordinates and arc type specifications to demonstrate CHORD and OPEN arcs.

*These graphics are drawn on a panel by a **paintComponent()** method – like the example on page 151.*

Drawing polygons

Polygons can be created with the **GeneralPath()** constructor method that is contained in the **java.awt.geom** class.

To make this method available to a program requires that the header statement **import java.awt.geom.*;** is added.

A **GeneralPath** object is used to store a number of points that define the shape of a polygon to be drawn by a program.

Once this object has been created its **moveTo()** method takes two arguments to set the first XY coordinate point.

Subsequent points are added with its **lineTo()** method that also takes two arguments to specify their XY coordinates.

Each successive point is added as XY coordinate arguments to the **lineTo()** method until all points have been set.

Finally the **GeneralPath** object's **closePath()** method should be called to connect the final point to the first point – and so complete the shape.

The example below replaces the **paintComponent()** method statements on page 151 to illustrate a triangular polygon:

DrawPolygon.java
(part of)

```
Graphics2D painter2D = (Graphics2D) painter;
painter2D.drawString("Polygon Triangle", 20, 25);
GeneralPath triangle = new GeneralPath();
triangle.moveTo(140F,20F);
triangle.lineTo(100F,65F);
triangle.lineTo(180F,65F);
triangle.closePath();
painter2D.fill(triangle);
```

This example fills the polygon but if drawn it would have a 1-pixel outline.

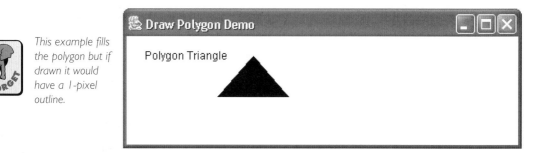

Working with files

This chapter illustrates how Java programs can utilize other external files, such as text files, sound files and image files. Examples demonstrate reading and writing with a text file, playing a sound file and adding images to an application.

Covers

Chapter Fourteen

Creating file objects

Java contains a class named **java.io** that is designed to handle file input and output procedures.

This class can be made available to a program by including a header statement of **import java.io.*;**.

The **java.io** package contains a class named **File** that can be used to access files or complete folders.

A **File** object is created with the Java "new" keyword and takes the file, or folder, name as its constructor argument.

For instance, the constructor creating a **File** object to represent a local file named **info.dat** would look like this:

```
File info = new File( "info.dat" );
```

Remember to surround the file name with double quotes.

This file could be either an existing file or a new file and the argument could include a path in the file name.

Note that the creation of a **File** object does not actually create a new file but merely a means to represent a file.

Once created, the **File** object has several useful methods that can be used to manipulate the actual file.

This table lists some of the common **File** object methods:

Method	Returns
exists()	true if the file exists – false if it does not
getName()	the file name as a String
length()	number of bytes in the file, as a long type
createNewFile()	true if able to create the new unique file
delete()	true if able to successfully delete the file
renameTo(File)	true if able to successfully rename the file
list()	an array of file or folder names as Strings

Listing files in a folder

The **list()** method of a **File** object can be used to list the names of all files and sub-folders contained in a folder.

This method returns the file names as a list of strings that can be assigned to a String[] array.

The files will not be listed in any particular order.

The array's length property contains an integer value of the total number of files found and this can be used in a loop to write a list of all the file names.

It is always good practice when dealing with files to allow the program an alternative if the file cannot be found.

The program below seeks a folder named "data" then lists the number of files found and their names:

data

dexter.bmp

oscar.txt

```java
import java.io.*;
public class ListFiles
{
  public static void main(String[] args)
  {
    File dir = new File("data");
    if(dir.exists())
    {
     String[] files = dir.list();
     System.out.println(files.length+" files found...");
     for(int i=0; i< files.length; i++)
     System.out.println(files[i]);
    }
    else System.out.println("Folder not found");
  }
}
```

```
Output Panel                                          ☒
  Starting application C:\MyJava\ListFiles.class    ▲
  2 files found...
  dexter.bmp
  oscar.txt
  Interactive Session Ended
  |                                                 ▼
 ⏮ ◀ ▶ ⏭ \ Results / Build \ Debug / ◀ |          ▶
```

Reading and writing files

The **java.io** package contains a class named **FileReader** that is especially designed to read from text files.

A **FileReader** object is created with the Java "new" keyword and takes the name of the file to be read as its argument.

When working with external files use a try-catch block in case of errors.

This object is just a representation of the file to be read.

Contents of the file can then be read into a **BufferedReader** object that specifies the **FileReader** object in its constructor.

The contents in the **BufferedReader** object can be accessed one line at a time with its **readLine()** method as shown here:

ReadFile.java

```
import java.io.*;
public class ReadFile
{
  public static void main(String[] args)
  {
    try
    {
      FileReader file=new FileReader("data/oscar.txt");
      BufferedReader buffer=new BufferedReader(file);

      String textline = null;
      while((textline = buffer.readLine()) != null)
      System.out.println(textline);
      buffer.close();
    }
    catch( IOException e ) { System.out.println(e); }
  }
}
```

*Remember to finally close the BufferedReader using its **close()** method.*

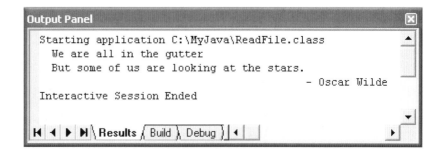

Output Panel

```
Starting application C:\MyJava\ReadFile.class
  We are all in the gutter
  But some of us are looking at the stars.
                                    - Oscar Wilde

Interactive Session Ended
```

Results / Build \ Debug

The **FileReader** and **BufferedReader** classes that can be used to read text files have counterparts named **FileWriter** and **BufferedWriter** that can be used to write text files.

A file name, and optionally a path, is specified as the argument to the **FileWriter** constructor method.

When working with external files use a try-catch block in case of errors.

In turn the new **FileWriter** object is specified as the argument to the **BufferedWriter** constructor method.

Now the **write()** method of the **BufferedWriter** object takes a String argument that will be written to the named text file.

The program below illustrates this procedure and also uses a **BufferedReader newLine()** method to write on a new line:

WriteFile.java

Remember to finally close the **BufferedWriter** *using its* **close()** *method.*

```java
import java.io.*
public class WriteFile
{
  public static void main(String args[])
  {
    try
    {
      FileWriter file = new FileWriter("louis.txt");
      BufferedWriter buffer = new BufferedWriter(file);

      buffer.write("L'État c'est moi ");
      buffer.write("(I am the State)");
      buffer.newLine();
      buffer.write("... Louis XIV");
      buffer.close();
    }
    catch (IOException e) { System.out.println(e); }
  }
}
```

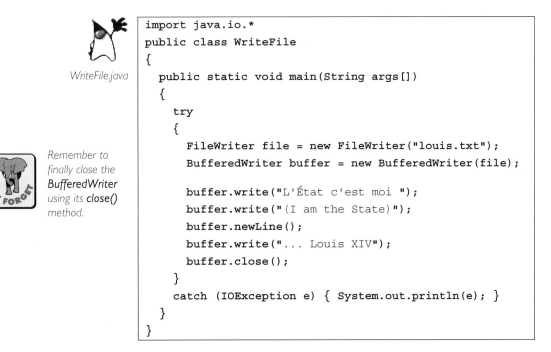

louis.txt

```
louis.txt - Notepad
File  Edit  Format  View  Help
L'État c'est moi (I am the State)
... Louis XIV
```

Adding images

In order to add a GIF or JPEG image to an interface an **Image** object must first be created to store the image details.

For applets the **JApplet** class has a method named **getImage()** that is used to create an **Image** object. This method takes two arguments to specify the location and name of an image.

See page 138 for an example applet that adds an image.

The location can be specified as an absolute URL or simply with the **getCodeBase()** method if the image file is contained in the same folder as the applet file.

For applications the **Abstract Windowing Toolkit** class has a **getImage()** method that is contained in its **Toolkit** class and is made available by its **getDefaultToolkit()** method.

In both applets and applications the Image object is applied with the **drawImage()** method of a **Graphics** context.

Remember to include the "if" statement shown here to ensure that the Image is available to draw.

This method takes four arguments that specify the **Image** object, XY coordinates at which to draw the image, and finally the "this" keyword to keep track of image updates.

The code below could be added to the **paintComponent()** method on page 151 to illustrate how to add an image:

AddImages.java (part of)

```
Image pic =
    Toolkit.getDefaultToolkit().getImage("deedee.gif");
if(pic != null) painter.drawImage(pic, 15, 5, this);
```

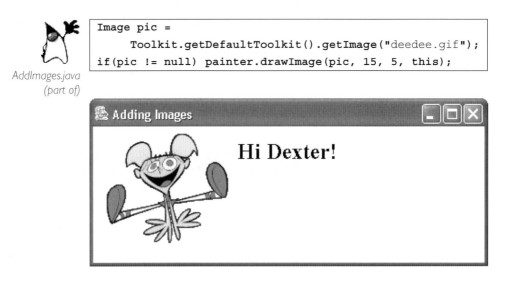

Using an **ImageIcon** object is a simple way to add GIF or JPEG images to Swing components and is to be encouraged.

An **ImageIcon** object is created with the Java "new" keyword and its constructor method specifies an **Image** object.

Once created, the **ImageIcon** object can be added to **JLabel** and **JButton** components by specifying the **ImageIcon** name as the argument to the component's constructor method.

Images that are placed in the same folder as the Java files can be referred to without including a path.

The **JButton** constructor may have two arguments to specify both an **ImageIcon** and a String to appear on the button.

When the program renders the component it will include the images as a fixed part of that component.

If the specified image files are not located the component is displayed without the image and no error message occurs.

The code listed below creates a **JLabel** component and two **JButton** components that incorporate **ImageIcons**:

*ImgIcon.java
(part of)*

```
Image dex = getImage( getCodeBase(),"dexter.gif" );
  ImageIcon dexter = new ImageIcon( dex );
   JLabel label = new JLabel( dexter );
Image yes = getImage( getCodeBase(),"accept.gif" );
  ImageIcon tick = new ImageIcon( yes );
   JButton accept = new JButton( "Accept", tick );
Image no = getImage( getCodeBase(),"cancel.gif" );
  ImageIcon cross = new ImageIcon( no );
   JButton cancel = new JButton( "Cancel", cross );
```

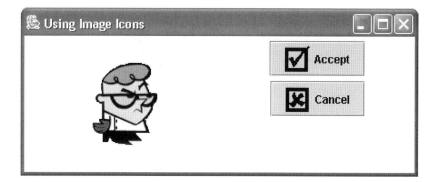

Applications with sound

Java applications can be made to play sound files that are in the format of AU, AIFF, WAV or MIDI file types.

Sound capability is provided by a class named **AudioClip** that is part of the **JApplet** class.

It is not necessary to create a JApplet object to play sounds.

This can be made available to a program with the header statement **import java.applet.AudioClip;**.

An **AudioClip** object has methods named **play()**, **loop()** and **stop()** which are used to handle sound files.

A sound may play once with the **play()** method or repeatedly with **loop()** and can be silenced using the **stop()** method.

The **AudioClip()** constructor method takes a URL object as its argument stating the address of an actual sound file to play and has the following syntax:

```
AudioClip theSound = new AudioClip( theURL );
```

The URL class is part of the java.net package that is added to a program with the header statement **import java.net.*;**.

Its constructor method takes the sound file's address as its argument and local files can be stated with the "file:" protocol specifier using this syntax:

```
URL soundFile = new URL( "file:sound.wav" );
```

For more on adding a MouseListener interface see page 130.

When using the URL class its constructor must always be enclosed in a try-catch block to handle address errors.

These are called **MalformedURLException** exceptions.

The **mousePressed()** event handler shown on the facing page creates two **AudioClip** objects.

This event handler can be called by two **JLabel** components that have **ImageIcons** and **MouseListeners** added.

When the user clicks the mouse on one of these **JLabel** components the program will play the appropriate sound.

PlaySounds.java
(part of)

The JLabels in this example are named "playBeep" and "playBell".

```java
public void mousePressed(MouseEvent event)
{
  try
  {
    URL beepFile = new URL( "file:beep.wav" );
    AudioClip beep = JApplet.newAudioClip( beepFile );

    URL ringFile = new URL( "file:ring.wav" );
    AudioClip ring = JApplet.newAudioClip( ringFile );

    if( event.getSource() == playBeep ) beep.play();
    if( event.getSource() == playBell ) ring.play();
  }
  catch( MalformedURLException error ){ }
}

// required empty MouseListener event handlers
public void mouseReleased( MouseEvent event ){ }
public void mouseClicked( MouseEvent event ){ }
public void mouseEntered( MouseEvent event ){ }
public void mouseExited( MouseEvent event ){ }
```

Applets with sound

The applet shown below uses the same technique as the previous example to create an **AudioClip** object. The sound plays repeatedly until a Stop button is pressed:

SoundApplet.java

All the classes used here were also needed in the previous example.

The URL constructor can specify the absolute location of a sound file as its argument.

```java
import java.applet.*;
import java.awt.event.*;
import java.awt.*;
import java.net.*;
import javax.swing.*;

public class SoundApplet extends JApplet
                                  implements ActionListener
{
  URL sound; AudioClip music;
  public void init()
  {
    try
    {  sound = new URL("file:music.wav");
       music = JApplet.newAudioClip(sound);
       music.loop();
    }
    catch(MalformedURLException error){}
    Container contentArea = getContentPane();
    JButton button = new JButton("Click To Stop Sound");
    button.addActionListener(this);
    contentArea.add(button);
  }

  public void actionPerformed(ActionEvent event)
  { music.stop(); }
}
```

Threads and animation

This chapter illustrates how program threads can be used to produce timers that perform tasks at specified intervals. Examples demonstrate timers in action with a Java clock and an animation sequence. There is also explanation of archive files, and how to go further in Java programming.

Covers

Chapter Fifteen

Creating a thread

Threads can be used in a Java program to allow it to perform several tasks simultaneously. This technique is called "multi-tasking" and is achieved by performing each task within its own individual thread.

Each Thread object can be created in Java using the **Thread** class that is part of the **java.lang** package of classes. A program must also have the **Runnable** interface from the same package to control the performance of a **Thread**. As the **java.lang** classes are permanently available to all programs no special import statements are needed.

The **Runnable** interface is made available to a program with the "implements" keyword in the class declaration.

A **Thread** object can be declared at the start of a program so instances of the **Thread** may be created as the program runs:

```
Thread runner;
```

Threads are also useful to prevent delays in execution of a program by allowing multi-tasking.

Threads have a useful method named **sleep()** that allows the execution of the **Thread** to be paused for a specified time.

Typically this is used in animations where several images are displayed in sequence to create the illusion of movement. The delay between images can be controlled by specifying a millisecond value as the argument to the **sleep()** method.

If the program cannot pause for the specified delay an **InterruptedException** will occur so the **sleep()** method should always be called from inside a **try-catch** block.

This example first calls a method named **repaint()** then pauses a **Thread** named "runner" for a delay of one second:

```
try
{
  repaint();
  runner.sleep( 1000 );
}
catch (InterruptedException e ) { }
```

In order to run a **Thread** the **Runnable** interface should be added to a Java program with the "implements" keyword.

All programs that implement the **Runnable** interface must include a method named **run()** to define the task that a **Thread** should perform.

The **run()** method should first ensure that the **Thread** exists using the **Thread.currentThread()** method like this example:

```java
Thread runner;

public void run()
{
  while ( runner == Thread.currentThread() )
  {
    repaint();
    try { Thread.sleep(1000); }
    catch( InterruptedException e ) {}
  }
}
```

A program could call these start() or stop() methods as often as required to execute the run() method and its defined task.

This method is never called directly but calling the Thread's **start()** method will execute the defined **run()** method task.

Before calling the Thread's **start()** method the program must ensure that the **Thread** is not already running by making a comparison to a **null** value like this:

```java
public void start()
{
  if(runner == null) runner = new Thread(this);
  runner.start();
}
```

Similarly a **Thread** can be halted by setting its value to **null**:

These examples are used in the Java clock program on the next page.

```java
public void stop()
{
  if(runner != null) runner = null;
}
```

Java Clock program

This program uses the **Calendar** class of the **java.util** package to retrieve information about the current system time.

The program's constructor method calls a **start()** method that sets a **Thread** running to repaint a panel every second.

Clock.java

```java
import java.awt.*;  /* Import required classes */
import javax.swing.*;
import java.util.*;

class Clock extends JFrame implements Runnable
{
```

Declare global objects
```java
  Thread runner;
  Font clockFont;
```

```java
  public Clock()
  {
```

Create the window
```java
    super("Java Clock"); setSize(300, 100);
    setDefaultCloseOperation(JFrame.EXIT_ON_CLOSE);
    setVisible(true);
```

Create the Font instance
```java
    clockFont= new Font("Serif", Font.BOLD, 40);
```

Add the components
```java
    Container contentArea = getContentPane();
    ClockPanel timeDisplay = new ClockPanel();
    contentArea.add(timeDisplay);
    setContentPane(contentArea);
```

Start the Thread running
```java
    start();
  }
```

```java
  class ClockPanel extends JPanel
  {
    public void paintComponent(Graphics painter)
    {
```

Create a clock component
```java
      painter.setColor(Color.white);
      painter.fillRect(0,0,300,100);
      painter.setFont(clockFont);
      painter.setColor(Color.red);
      painter.drawString( timeNow(), 60, 40);
    }
}
```

Clock.java (cont'd)

```java
public String timeNow()
{
  Calendar now = Calendar.getInstance();
  int hrs = now.get(Calendar.HOUR_OF_DAY);
  int min = now.get(Calendar.MINUTE);
  int sec = now.get(Calendar.SECOND);
  String time = zero(hrs)+":"+zero(min)+":"+zero(sec);
  return time;
}
```

Get the current time

```java
public String zero(int num)
{
  String number=( num < 10 ) ? ("0"+num) : (""+num);
  return number;
}
```

Add leading zero if needed

```java
public void start()
{
  if(runner == null) runner = new Thread(this);
  runner.start();
}
```

Method to start Thread

```java
public void run()
{
  while (runner == Thread.currentThread() )
  {
    repaint();
    try { Thread.sleep(1000); }
    catch(InterruptedException e) {}
  }
}
```

Define the Thread task

```java
public static void main(String[] args)
{ Clock eg = new Clock(); }
}
```

Program's main method

Java Clock

13:09:30

Animation with Java

All animation relies upon the rapid replacement of images with others that are slightly different to the previous image.

If the speed at which the images are replaced is fast enough this technique creates the illusion of actual movement.

For instance, the frames of a movie film are just images that are replaced in quick succession to create a motion picture.

Java 2 Swing components run flicker-free animations without the double-buffering techniques needed in earlier versions.

Similarly a Java **Thread** has the ability to repaint a Swing component in rapid succession with a sequence of images.

The resulting appearance is like the animated GIF files which are widely used on many web pages.

But the Java animation has some additional features:

1   A Java animation **Thread** can be stopped and restarted by calling its **start()** method or setting the **Thread** to **null**.

2   A Java animation can also play sound by calling **play()** and **stop()** methods of an **AudioClip** object.

3   A Java animation can respond to user events by calling event handler methods in the program.

4   A Java applet animation can be easily customized by changing its parameter values.

5   A Java animation can comprise purely graphics drawn by the **Graphics** context in the program.

So Java animations can offer greater flexibility to the developer in a wide variety of different circumstances.

The technique that is used to create Java animations was also used in the Java **Clock** program on the previous pages.

In that case the program was replacing the clock numerals at one-second intervals but the same principle is used to replace images at shorter intervals to create animation.

Images that are to be used in Java animations are best created in the popular GIF file format which is compact and also allows for areas of the image to be transparent.

The images should be made in a graphics application with layering capability, such as Photoshop or Paint Shop Pro.

On the bottom layer create all the static parts of the image that will not change during the animation sequence.

Add extra layers for each part of the image to be animated.

When all layers and images are complete the file can be saved as the first image "frame" in the animation sequence.

The elements of the image that are to be animated can then be modified on their own separate layers to change their position, color and size until the desired effect is reached.

Now the modified image file can be saved with a different file name to become the second frame in the animation.

This procedure can be repeated as many times as necessary to create all the frames that are needed in the animation.

The illustration shown to the left on this page is the first frame of an animation that will be created in this chapter.

It has separate layers for the juggler's eyes, hands, left foot and each juggling ball – all of these will be animated by changing their position to make a sequence of five frames.

The images are saved as separate GIF files named **image0, image1, image2, image3, image4** and are illustrated below:

Loading animation images

A sequence of images that are to be used in a Java animation should be assigned to an **Image[]** array starting at zero.

The **Image[]** array should first be declared as a class variable to be globally available to the program.

Image files can be assigned to the array's elements by an applet's **init()** method, or the constructor in an application.

Typically a loop is used to fill the elements sequentially.

In applets the image file names can be specified in the HTML code as parameter values to be retrieved by the loop.

The **getParameter()** method in the loop example shown below retrieves five image file values from parameters which are named **img0, img1, img2, img3** and **img4**.

If the images are located the images are assigned by the loop to sequential elements of an **Image[]** array named "pic".

A variable counter keeps track of the total number of images.

The image files created on the previous page are assigned as the parameter values in the HTML code.

```
Image[] pic = new Image[5];
int total = 0;

public void init()
{
  for(int i = 0; i < 5; i++)
  {
    String imgRef = null;
    imgRef = getParameter("img"+i);
    if(imgRef != null)
    {
      pic[i] = getImage(getCodeBase(), imgRef);
      total++;
    }
  }
}
```

This code forms part of the Juggler applet which is listed in full over the next three pages to illustrate an animation that can be started and stopped by pushing interface buttons.

Java Juggler applet

Juggler.java

```java
import java.awt.*;  /* Import required classes */
import java.awt.event.*;
import javax.swing.*;

public class Juggler extends JApplet
                          implements Runnable, ActionListener
{
```

Declare globals for Thread, buttons, image array and counter variables

```java
  Thread runner;
  JButton play;
  JButton stop;
  Image[] pic = new Image[5];
  int total = 0;
  int count = 0;
```

```java
  public void init()
  {
```

Load images specified in the HTML parameters into the image array

```java
    for(int i=0; i<5; i++)
    {
      String img = null;
      img = getParameter("image"+i);
      if(img != null)
      {
       pic[i] = getImage(getCodeBase(), img);
        total++;
      }
    }
```

Create the main container

```java
    Container contentArea = getContentPane();
    GridLayout grid = new GridLayout(1,2);
    contentArea.setLayout(grid);
    contentArea.setBackground(Color.white);
```

Create the animation panel

```java
    JugglerPanel animation = new JugglerPanel();
```

Create console panel for text label and buttons

```java
    JPanel console = new JPanel();
    FlowLayout flow = new FlowLayout();
    console.setLayout(flow);
    console.setBackground(Color.white);
```

Create label component complete with ImageIcon

```java
    Image signImage = getImage(getCodeBase(),"sign.gif");
    ImageIcon signIcon = new ImageIcon(signImage);
    JLabel sign = new JLabel(signIcon);
```

Juggler.java
(cont'd)

Create button components
complete with ImageIcons and
ActionListeners

```java
Image playImage=getImage(getCodeBase(),"accept.gif");
ImageIcon playIcon = new ImageIcon(playImage);
play = new JButton("Click To Start", playIcon);
play.addActionListener(this);

Image stopImage=getImage(getCodeBase(),"cancel.gif");
ImageIcon stopIcon = new ImageIcon(stopImage);
stop = new JButton("Click To Stop", stopIcon);
stop.addActionListener(this);
```

Add the components

```java
console.add(sign);
console.add(play); console.add(stop);
contentArea.add(animation);
contentArea.add(console);
setContentPane(contentArea);
}
```

Event handler for buttons
to start or stop animation

```java
public void actionPerformed(ActionEvent event)
{
  if(event.getSource() == stop) stop();
  if(event.getSource() == play) start();
}
```

Paint the animation panel

```java
class JugglerPanel extends JPanel
{
  public void paintComponent(Graphics painter)
  {
    if( pic[count] != null )
    painter.drawImage( pic[count], 0, 0,this);
  }
}
```

Thread starter method

```java
public void start()
{
  if(runner == null)
  {
    runner = new Thread(this);
    runner.start();
  }
}
```

Thread stopper method

```java
public void stop()
{ if(runner != null) runner = null; }
```

Juggler.java (cont'd)

Thread task to repaint the animation and increment the image counter

```java
public void run()
  {
    while (runner == Thread.currentThread() )
    {
      repaint();
      count++;
      if(count >= total) count=0;
      try
      {
      Thread.sleep(100);
      }
      catch(InterruptedException e) {}
    }
  }
}
```

The applet will run the animation automatically when it is opened but it can be stopped and restarted with the buttons.

*Applets will automatically call the **start()** method, right after they have called the **init()** method, when they are first loaded.*

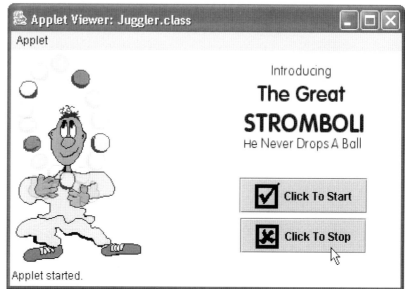

Java archive files

The Java SDK includes a tool named "jar" that can be used to package all the files used by an applet into a single file.

This new file will have the extension ".jar" and can include sound and image files along with the applet's own class files.

The Java archive (jar) file will also benefit from compression that reduces the download time needed to run the applet.

Just type "jar" at a command prompt to see options for the jar tool.

If the applet has been initially developed to load files from HTML parameter values, the applet code can be changed to load the images directly from the jar file using this syntax:

```
getImage( getClass().getResource( "imagename.gif" ) );
```

To prepare the Java Juggler applet to use a jar file for all its image and class files would first require its code to be amended to load all its image files direct from the jar file.

These amendments apply to loading the animation images and images for button and label components.

The revised **init()** method and constructors look like this:

These pieces of code can replace their counterparts in the Juggler applet code listed on the previous pages.

```java
public void init()
{
  for( int i=0; i<5; i++ )
  {
    pic[i] =
    getImage( getClass().getResource("image"+i+".gif") );
    total++;
  }
}

Image signImage =
  getImage( getClass().getResource("sign.gif") );

Image playImage =
  getImage( getClass().getResource("accept.gif") );

Image stopImage =
  getImage( getClass().getResource("cancel.gif") );
```

HTMLConverter can add code that forces the browser to use the Java 2 plug-in – see page 143.

Now all the **<param>** tags can be removed from the HTML code because they are no longer used to specify image files. The **<applet>** tag must retain its "code" attribute and add an "archive" attribute to which is assigned the jar file name – the revised **<applet>** tag looks like this:

```
<applet code="Juggler.class" archive="Juggler.jar"
                          width="300" height="230" >
```

The jar tool is a command-line application that uses this syntax to create a new Java archive jar file:

```
jar cvf JAR-filename list-of-files
```

In the above command "cvf" tells the jar tool to create a new archive file and confirm the result of its operation.

All of the files used by the Juggler applet are shown below:

Notice that inner classes are created as a separate file – remember to include these in the jar file.

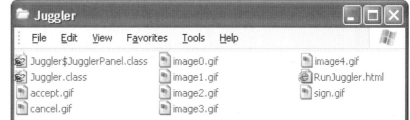

These image and class files can be incorporated into a jar file named **Juggler.jar** as a list of files with a command like this:

```
C:\MyJava>jar cvf Juggler.jar Juggler.class sign.gif
```

Once a jar file has been created, further files can be added to it with a similar command that uses "uvf" in place of "cvf". This tells the jar tool to update the archive file with a list of files and confirm the result of its operation. When all the Juggler files have been added into the **Juggler.jar** archive, opening the **RunJuggler.html** document will run the applet using the archived images.

Listing and extracting jar contents

Java archive (jar) files provide a convenient way of supplying support files to an applet in a compressed single file. This has the added advantage of making the individual files difficult to access by anyone unable to extract each file.

The Java SDK jar tool can extract all files in a jar archive by using this instruction at the command prompt:

```
jar xvf JAR-filename
```

Some jar archives contain very many files so it may be preferable to inspect the contents of the archive and then only extract files of particular interest. The instruction to list the archive's contents uses "tvf" in place of "xvf" in the command shown above.

Viewing the contents of the **Juggler.jar** archive file created on the previous page produces the results below:

The jar archive in this example achieved a total reduction in file size of 20%.

```
Command Prompt                              _ □ ✕

C:\MyJava>jar tvf Juggler.jar
       0 Sat Apr 21 12:32:44 EDT 2005 META-INF/
      68 Sat Apr 21 12:32:44 EDT 2005 META-INF/MANIFE
    3121 Sat Apr 21 13:03:56 EDT 2005 Juggler.class
     626 Sat Apr 21 12:30:10 EDT 2005 Juggler$Juggler
    3245 Fri Apr 20 14:15:52 EDT 2005 sign.gif
    3341 Thu Apr 19 18:21:02 EDT 2005 image0.gif
    3719 Thu Apr 19 18:21:40 EDT 2005 image1.gif
    3402 Thu Apr 19 18:22:02 EDT 2005 image2.gif
    3373 Thu Apr 19 18:22:26 EDT 2005 image3.gif
    3375 Thu Apr 19 18:22:58 EDT 2005 image4.gif
     945 Thu Apr 19 12:53:44 EDT 2005 accept.gif
     938 Thu Apr 19 12:56:52 EDT 2005 cancel.gif
```

The first two files listed are part of every jar archive and just contain meta information about its contents.

An individual file can be extracted from the archive by adding the required file name to the "xvf" command above.

So a command to extract the bottom image file would be:

```
C:\MyJava>jar xvf Juggler.jar cancel.gif
```

Generating program documentation

The Java SDK contains a fantastic program named "javadoc" that can automatically generate program documentation. A whole series of linked HTML files are generated that detail the class declarations and methods in the program.

Comments added to the source files of a program will be included in the HTML documentation if they were added using a comment style recognized by **javadoc**. This comment style precedes comments with /** and terminates the comment with */.

Include HTML tags in comments to format the comment in the output documentation.

Although code in this book is uncommented to save space it's good style to include comments in all programs to help understanding of the code. For instance, this comment could be added before the **JugglerPanel** class declaration in the **Juggler** applet:

```
/** The JugglerPanel class provides an area
 *   in the applet interface on which to display
 *   an animated sequence of GIF images.
 */
```

The **javadoc** program can be run from within the JPadPro IDE by selecting the JDK menu option then **Run Javadoc**.

Javadoc can be run from a command prompt with this syntax:

```
javadoc JAVA-filename
```

Running **javadoc** with the **Juggler.java** file creates HTML documentation describing the **Juggler** applet and includes the recognized comment about the **JugglerPanel class**:

```
: Class Juggler.JugglerPanel
  File   Edit   View   Favorites   Tools   Help

  class Juggler.JugglerPanel
  extends javax.swing.JPanel

  The JugglerPanel class provides an area in the applet interface
  on which to display an animated sequence of GIF images.

                                        My Computer
```

Java SDK documentation

The format of the program documentation that is generated by **javadoc** follows that used for the SDK documentation.

Having gained some experience with the Java language it is now useful to obtain the main SDK documentation. This is available from the documentation download page on Sun Microsystems' website at **http://java.sun.com/docs**.

Standard documentation is in HTML format and the single download zip package weighs in at around 35 MB. Notice that the size of the documentation, even in this compressed form, indicates how large the Java language is.

The documentation can be downloaded in smaller pieces but these cannot be viewed until the total number of files have been downloaded.

Alternatively, the SDK documentation is available in a ported version using the WinHelp format for Windows platforms. This is a single zip package of around 29 MB that can be downloaded from **http://www.confluent.fr/javadoc**.

Although this format is familiar, it is generally preferable to download the HTML documentation and install it in a folder named "docs" in the SDK directory. The file named "index.html" that gets installed in this folder is the starting point for the entire documentation package.

The SDK documentation can reference other parts of the SDK when installed in HTML format.

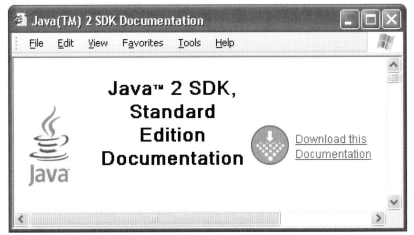

Opening the index file for the SDK documentation reveals an Overview page that gives information about many different aspects of the Java 2 language possibilities.

Of primary interest on this page is the link to the Java 2 Platform API Specification that provides details of all the main class packages that are available in the Java 2 SDK.

At the top of this page are a number of menu links.

The "Index" menu link on this page will open a page that details all the Java classes, sub classes and methods that begin with the letter "A".

The entire range of SDK classes and methods are listed in the documentation in alphabetical order and can be accessed by their starting letter through the alphabet menu at the top of each of those pages.

These alphabetical listings are most useful and it is convenient to make a desktop shortcut to one of these pages.

The SDK documentation can almost seem like too much detail – but it does ensure that you will find what you need.

In JPadPro a link to an alphabetical documentation page can also be added to the Help window that has a "?" on its tab in the Workspace Panel.

This allows the SDK documentation to be readily viewed in the main window of the JPadPro IDE.

Other menu links at the top of the documentation pages named Package, Class, Use and Tree give information about the hierarchical relationship between classes and methods.

A further menu link gives details of parts of Java that have been deprecated to become obsolete in the current version.

Clicking on any class or method anywhere in the SDK documentation will lead to further information about that item, its use and its parent class.

Become accustomed to using the SDK documentation frequently to further your understanding of the Java language and how it is arranged in class hierarchies.

Java resources

This book will, hopefully, have provided you with a great introduction to Java programming and may have whetted your appetite to find out even more.

The Java phenomenon has been largely spread via the Internet which has spawned a host of online Java resources.

When seeking the latest news about Java the first place to look should always be the Sun Microsystems website.

New versions of the Java SDK and other programming resources are available for free download here.

http://java.sun.com

There are numerous avenues to explore on the Sun website relating to the emerging technologies that will see Java used in appliances such as cellphones, TVs and even refrigerators.

A number of discussion groups are also available here with help for all Java programmers from beginner to expert.

Details about the Sun Certified Programmer certification are given for those interested in a career in Java programming.

Another terrific online Java resource is the Java Applet Rating Service that reviews the latest applets on the web.

http://www.jars.com

Applets are rated as being Top 1%, Top 5% or Top 25%, according to how good they are.

The source code for many of the featured applets is available for download and this is useful to examine how the Java code has been written.

http://www.javaworld.com

For news and views on Java development the JavaWorld online magazine is highly recommended.

This website is updated monthly with all the latest news and frequently features tutorial articles that are able to discuss a topic then demonstrate it with an applet online.

Investigation of the Java resources available for free on the Internet should ensure that there is no shortage of help to advance your Java skills – Happy Programming!

Index

R

S

T

U